'Get me out

Based on a true story
Written by Elisa Singh Teulings

Cover : Elisa Singh
www.elisasingh-teulings.com

All rights reserved.

No part of this publication may be reproduced or made public through printing, photocopying,
microfilm or in any other way, without
written permission from the author.

Secretly, I'm dying inside.
Wearing my mask to hide
The torture, the pain
My head is going insane.
I feel nothing no more.
Except for grief and sorrow
I don't want to live.
I don't want to wake up tomorrow.
Nobody noticed the fight.
Against these demons inside
All because of my beautiful mask to hide
Don't tell me everything is going to be okay.
Just hug me and understand
Don't leave me, and please stay.
Nobody knows nobody shall see
How my childhood is secretly killing me

- Elisa Singh

Intuition

I can directly see if there has been an abuse of a child.
As soon as I'm meeting everyone who immerses in the room and makes contact with the child, I first win their trust, and not much later, the secret gently soaks. In the knowledge that there are still children in fear and uncertainty, life gives me sleepless nights.
My passionate desire to reach out for these children and to offer a helping hand is growing stronger by the day.
Now that I have become a mother of three beautiful children, I don't understand people who use any form of violence against children. How can you damage or humiliate an innocent child? What kind of sick minds feel capable of doing that to a child?

No one who sees it, notice, or hear. Everyone is busy in life. We also don't want to interfere with someone's life. We have a fear of getting blamed for interference.
The beast carries a mask, disguised as the friendly neighbor, a loving mother, a concerned coach, or an overprotective relative.
No one notices how bad they are. Those persons use the weakness and the loyalty of a child. It leaves deep traces, and they are not all visible to the outside world.

The self-loathing and disgust reflect in the eyes. Confidence in man is ruined, which causes many problems later in life.
The fear to completely open up to the people around you hampers you to enjoy the moment because the fear of getting hurt prevails.
The wall around your heart is getting higher, and it is becoming increasingly difficult for your loved ones to come through it.
Lifelong damage because of what they have done to you. Monsters you trusted that you thought you loved, they have destroyed you. Will this hell pass?

There sounds a deathly silence.
Internal scream: Get me out of here!

29 November 1990

That conscious morning, it had been snowing in the night. The house felt cold, and her mother was still asleep on the leather sofa in the living room. On her bare feet, she came gently closer.
'Mommy?' She tried to rouse her gently. She had about ten minutes to reach school on time and still had to eat breakfast.
'Go to sleep,' muttered her mother irritated and turned around.
Mum had poorly slept again last night, she thought, and she decided to look for something to eat by herself.
Her rumbling stomach went on a rampage as an autumn-like thunderstorm.
The breakfast played through her mind when she heard Robbie waking up. She ran into their bedroom. He cast a friendly smile on her.
'Have you slept well?' she asked her little brother.
He paused and pulled on to the bars of his crib.
Elisa gently lifted her little brother out of his cot, ran to the kitchen, and put Robbie in his high chair. Robbie was not so big, but it took her a lot of trouble. Between the tall piles of dishes on the kitchen counter, she found his drinking bottle. The milk from the day before was still in it. She looked at it and pulled her nose up.
'Blegh, so dirty.'
With arms outstretched, she changed the cover losses.

As soon as she opens the bottle, she smells sour air.
She quickly flushed the retching bottle with hot water, but it was not helping very much. The smell was unbearable, and also, with dish soap, she didn't get the stench off.
'You need to drink from a normal cup, like a big boy.'
She moved a kitchen chair against the sink block and climbed up. When she stood on her toes, she could just reach the cups that were behind in the upper kitchen cabinet.
Robbie followed every movement of his big sister.
From the living room, they heard soft moans. It was their mother who had turned around again. There was not much food available, on an old slice of bread and the remaining leftovers jam in a glass jar that stood lonely in the empty fridge. She sighed; this was never enough for both of them.
She looked at Robbie.
'Come on. We're going to eat, brother.'
She cut the sandwich carefully with a sharp knife into small pieces and gave these to the little Robbie.
When she looked at the clock, she saw that school had already started. She let out a deep sigh. Now the teacher will be mad at her again.
Her mother had woken up by the sounds that came out of the kitchen and came out to take a look.
'Did you still not leave for school?' she asked, surprised when she saw her children.

'No, Mommy, I was hungry and wanted to eat something first. But there is not enough, and Robbie has to eat too, so I gave him a sandwich. But now I'm late at school, the teacher will be angry at me,' she sighed.
'Hm, yes, that will do. Shoot but quickly, and then I'll give your little brother something to eat.'
Her mother searched her bag and pulled out a crumbled cookie, which was still in the packaging.
'Here, eat this and now quickly go to school.'
She felt her mother's warm lips on her crown when she put on her coat.
'Until this afternoon, mom.'
'See you soon, sweetie, I love you.'

Farewell

I was a studious child and went to school with a lot of fun. I felt terrible when I arrived late. My teacher's name was called Sophie, a beautiful woman of thirty-two years old. With her long red locks and thousands of freckles on her face, she looked lovely.

I think she loved flowers because she wore a beautiful dress with a floral design in Rainbow colors. I think she was lovely and funny. But if anyone was late in her classroom, her cheerful face changed into a dark stormy cloud. She did not like latecomers and not when you entered in the middle of a lesson.

The face of Miss Sophie spoke volumes when I entered the classroom.

I tried not to disturb the class and tried to reach my table as quietly as possible that stood behind in the classroom.

'Why are you so late, young lady?' She asked sternly.
'I am sorry, Miss. But I couldn't do anything about it. My mom was still sleeping when I woke up, and I needed to eat something first.'
A deep frown emerged on her forehead.
'Grab your work quickly from yesterday afternoon and finish this.'
She takes a banana from her desk drawer.
'Here, eat this.' With a wink, she handed over the banana.
'Thank you,' I whispered gratefully.

After I finished the banana, I started working. I had to draw lines between the images and the corresponding words.
I had no problem and finished my work on time. After that, it was time for the math lesson. Math was not my favorite subject in school, but I tried my best. My class consisted of fifteen children.
I didn't have any real friends. I didn't live so long at my mother's place. From my second to my fourth life year, I had temporarily lived with my aunt and uncle.

After the math lesson, we held a break. The children grabbed their bag off the coat rack in the hallway and brought them back into the classroom.
I was the only one who always remained seated. I had nothing in my bag that I could eat.
Miss Sophie distributed packs of school milk.
When she arrived at my desk, she stopped and gave me a sandwich of her own.
I think she smeared every day one extra, especially for me.
While I looked skittish around me, I felt so grateful. I ate the whole cheese sandwich. None of the children seemed to have noticed what was going on between the Miss and me. After we all finished our food and drinks, it was time to play outside. At the schoolyard, the children got divided into two groups. The girls started to build a snowman, while the boys ran behind each other and

threw snowballs. The screams and shouts of the children playing bounced between the outer walls of the school building.

I didn't care much for outdoor playing, and besides that, I didn't like the snow at all.

I preferred to stay inside and to draw something.

No blank sheet of paper was safe for me. I was pretty good at it too.

The day was mostly quiet and without problems. Once the school bell went, all the kids ran outside. There, their parents were waiting for them to take them home.

I felt invisible as I ran along with the crowd towards our apartment. It was not so far away. Our building was about seven hundred meters from my school.

We lived in an apartment, my mother, step-father, Robbie, and I. My step-father was the biological father of my little brother.

Not mine; my father lived with his wife somewhere else. I am living proof of an extramarital affair between my father and mother.

Even though there was an elevator, I preferred the stairs.

When I had reached our floor, I was out of breath. I had asthma, for which I had to take daily Ventolin. Because I had a fear of heights, I ran as close as possible along with the houses straight to ours.

I never dared to look down and took out a sigh every time I reached our threshold.

That was strange. The front door was open. Usually, I called my mother, and she would open the door. I pushed with my hand against the door and looked inside.

In the Hall were boxes and bags piled up against the wall. I saw my teddy bear and Robbie's sleeping bag.

What's going on here? I asked myself.

Are we going on a vacation?

'Mom, I'm home.'

I heard coughing from the living room.

My mother lay sprawled on the couch. Her face looked grizzled.

Robbie sat on the ground and was playing with his blocks. She was not alone.

In the window seat sat a lady who I had not seen before.

'Hi, sweetie. How was school?' asked mom with a trembling voice.

'Nice,' I muttered quietly. 'Have you been sick again?'

She sighed deeply. She looked so sad that particular day. I had never seen her down like that before.

My mother was twenty-five years old at that time—a beautiful young woman who drives men's minds crazy.

Long blonde hair. Mom had an open glance, beautiful long eyelashes, and a slim figure. She had a beautiful voice, which I could listen to for hours. She sang throughout the day, except at times when she lay down sick on the couch.

Her voice was like one of a princess; it sounded like angels were singing to my ears.

When she was in a good mood, she got up to dance to her favorite music. Then she grabbed my hands and danced around the living room with me. Our mother possessed no educational or parental qualities, but still, I loved her so deeply. These days, she gave us the attention and the care that we needed. On other days she lay in bed, there was no food in the house, and I didn't know what we had to eat. Then she gave the last bits to us, and she didn't eat anything herself. There was sometimes no warm water to take a bath in, or the tv stopped working. She did her best in her way. Given her past and youth, it was not so strange that she made bad choices in life. She didn't get a great example from her parents.

As I got older, I wondered why certain people get a child. If it were up to me, there would be extensive research to see if they are suitable as parents. In some cases, people don't think about it before they bring a child into this world.

Often in retrospect, it appears that their children's education is disappointing and heavier than they thought. Mostly this is at the expense of the children. They get taken away from home, and the absence of their parents is devastating. Each child who gets placed out of the house gets damaged for life.

Just the fact that they have to say goodbye to their parents and their familiar environment, leave deep traces in the children's soul.

The unknown woman held out her hand and introduced herself.
'Hi Elisa, how nice to meet you. My name is Nell.'
'What are you doing here?' I asked leery. I knew there was something wrong to expect.
With a calm voice, she told me the reason why she had come.
I could not believe it at first.
Does she want to take us away from our mother? Why?
'Mama, I don't want to leave home!'
I looked at her; she did not even look at me and avoided my gaze.
I saw that she did this to hide her tears.
'I am so sorry, sweetie. But I promise you that once mommy is better, I will take you home.'
Nell intervened, 'Don't promise her anything you can't make true.'
My mother got angry at her.
'Keep your mouth, woman! Don't you see how upset she is? The poor child. I try to calm her down.'
She turned back to me.
'Don't worry, Darling. I promise you'll quickly come home again, and then we will stay together forever.'

She could no longer restrain her tears and hold me tightly.

'Why are you sick? Can I still take care of you? Please let us stay here. I will do anything for you, whatever you want.

I am a sorry mommy if I've been naughty, and I promise you I will be from now on a good girl.' I begged, screamed, and cried, but nothing helped. We had to go away from our mother and our home.

'Now, we have to go,' said Nell, and she stood up.

Nell gloom, I mockingly thought. She can forget about it. I'm not coming with her.

'I'm not going!' I screamed and ran to my room.

It seemed as if I walked into a strange room. I saw my bed and the crib of Robbie, but there were no blankets on it. Our toys were gone, and the chest of drawers where typically our clothes lay in looked empty and plundered. In the corner of the upper drawer, I had found a candy bar that I had hidden during the summer holiday.

'Come on, sweetheart.' My mom stuck her head around the door and stepped in.

'Go away! I don't want to see you! Don't you love us anymore?'

'Yes, of course, sweetheart, but I can't do anything else. Mommy can't take care of your concerns at this moment. First, I need to get better, and I promise you that you will return to me. I promise you!'

I wanted to believe her. But I felt deeply hurt and lost at that time.

My throat hurts so much, and I want to stop crying. My cheeks stung by the salty tears that slide down my face.

Without saying anything, I walk along with my mother and Nell.

Nell carried Robbie on her arm to the elevator and pressed the button.

I wanted to last forever until the elevator came, but to my great disappointment, it lasted only a few seconds. Outside our flat stands a van.

While we said goodbye to our mother, Nell loaded all bags and boxes in her car. Nell put us in the back seat of the van, started the engine, and drove off.

Away from our home, our mother, and our familiar environment. I cried and thought about school. What would Miss Sophie think and say tomorrow morning if I did not show up? I didn't even get the chance to say goodbye to her.

I felt intense sadness. From that moment on, my whole life was upside down. Robbie had inherited nothing of what had just happened. Thank God he didn't understand it yet. Luckily though, I thought.

He looked so peaceful, with his eyes closed and sunk into a deep sleep.

Where would she take us? Is she going to bring us to my father?

We rode along with landmarks. It was the same route that my father drove when he came to pick me up for a weekend.

Nell struck left at the traffic lights where my dad always turns right. She didn't bring us to him.

The journey seemed to last an eternity.

'Does it take long?' I asked her.

'We are already there,' she replied and parked the car in a parking lot.

I looked outside and saw an apartment complex two stories high. 'Where are we?'

I felt my heart beating heavily in my chest. Robbie was still sleeping; his pacifier fell out of his mouth and lay on his lap.

'We are at your new home,' replied Nell while looking at us through the rearview mirror.

Your new home, well, that sounded weird to me.

My heart pounded faster. I was scared and had no idea what to expect. I didn't understand why all of a sudden, we had to leave our mother.

Didn't she love us anymore? Or did she have enough of us and wanted other kids?

A roller coaster of thoughts raged like a mad bull inside my little head.

'Heads up, don't worry. They are a lovely couple that will take good care of you and your little brother for as long as necessary,' she said, as she gently picked up the child seat Robbie was sleeping.

We got out and walked to the entrance of the building.
I looked at the names on all nameplates.
Nell pressed the little button of the family Blake, and after a few seconds, there was a female voice by the speaker, and the door opened for us.
'Come in,' said a lady with brown/red fluffy hair. A man with a beard and specs stood next to her.
I looked at them. The man wore a grey wool sweater and blue jeans and leaned on a wooden cane with one arm.
They also looked at me and smiled at me. In an attempt to smile at them back, I pulled my mouth corners a little up.
I had to wait on the couch in the living room and looked curious around me.
The living room had an old fashioned, velour sofa set, and there was an ugly painting against the yellowed wall. The yellowish color seemed to be smoke damage from nicotine.
On the floor lay a mouse grey carpeting; you saw small scuffs here and there. I looked again up to Nell and the unknown man and woman.
They were sitting at the glass kitchen table and looked our way now and then. Nell Vermaars spoke about half an hour with the people and then came to me.
'It is time to go now,' said Nell.
'I'm sure you are going to love it here.' She laughed and shook my hand. She left and left me along with my little brother behind. The Mrs. got up from her chair and

asked me to follow her to the room where I would sleep that night.
The apartment was on the ground floor and had three bedrooms at the end of the hallway. The room stood a bunk bed, a doll's house with a Barbie doll, and two small chairs. On the top bunk, there was a girl already sleeping; her name was Cindy.
She lived with her sister Kim also in this family.
The woman named Yolanda told me to put on my pajamas and to take place in the bed. It was already half-past seven in the evening. It was time to go to bed. I didn't mind this at all, because I was exhausted. But as soon as I laid down, I began to cry.
I missed my mother so much. Why didn't she want us anymore? What have I done wrong? I could only cry and called gently for my mother.
Cindy bent down over the edge of the bed and looked at me.
'Be quiet,' she whispered. 'You are not allowed to make a sound if you're in bed.'
'Sorry,' I whispered back. 'But I miss my mom so much.'
'I understand that, me too. But you have to be quiet. Otherwise, Yolanda will be angry at you.'
The door flew open, and Cindy flashed back in her bed.
'Who is crying here?' asked Yolanda.
'Me,' I answered.

20

'We have a rule here that once it is bedtime, everyone is silent, and I expect this from you too.' Her voice sounded imminent.

I was a little scared by her, pulled the covers a little further on to my chin, and said softly, 'I am sorry, Madam.'

'It's okay if you stop now and go to sleep.'

After these words, she closed the door behind her. After a while, I was still awake and stared at the bottom of the top bunk. Cindy seemed to be awake too.

Two legs slide down along the bed.

Cindy leaned over me to see if I was sleeping. I quickly squeezed my eyes tightly shut and pretended. I heard how she picked up something and started playing. Careful, I opened my eyes and lifted my head a bit up until I could see her. She was playing with the Doll House that stood in the room.

'What are you doing there?' I asked her.

She got scared, and the doll fell out of her hands.

'Shut your mouth,' she hissed with her finger to her mouth. 'Be quiet. Otherwise, they will hear us.'

It was too late.

We heard the living room door, and Cindy jumped back into her bed. With a jerk swung, our door went open, and Yolanda looked around the room like a mad bull.

'Who was out of bed?' She screamed wildly.

I wondered how it was even possible that they had heard her. Must she have supersonic ears like superheroes?

Cindy pretended she just woke up and denied that she was the one who got out of bed.
'Did you come out of your bed?' She asked me.
I shook my head. She grabbed my arm and dragged me out of bed. Cindy also got pulled out of the bed, and Yolanda took both of us to the living room.
'Someone was out that we heard, and I would now like to know who it was!'
I was shaking and looked at Cindy, who gave no reply and kept staring at the ground.

Peter, the master of the house, opened the sliding door that led into the garden. I felt the icy wind down my bare legs.
'If no one says something, then both of you stand outside. Until one of you has spoken the truth.'
They closed the sliding door and went to both sit on the couch.
I looked at Cindy, who kept staring at the ground in front of her. Initially, I didn't notice that we stood barefoot in the snow.
I felt the cold snow between my toes, and soon my feet started to tingle.
'Why don't you tell them the truth?'
'I'm scared,' she replied with a trembling voice.
It felt like hours, but it is hard to tell exactly how long we stood there.

I didn't hold on any longer. My whole body tingled, and I was shivering from the cold. I knocked on the window, and Peter shoved the door open.
'You remember already?'
I nodded. 'It was me,' I replied softly.
He threw his arm in the air with a large whisk, and before I could realize why he grabbed my hair and dragged me to the bathroom.
There he forced me to lean over the edge of the bath.
I cried and screamed.
'Don't! Please stop! It wasn't me …'
I felt a sharp pain in my back.
I screamed this time even harder. I peed in my pants out of fear. Again I felt how Peter hit me with something hard on my back. Before he hit me again, I saw the thing he hit me with, a brown leather belt with a large buckle. How many times Peter has beaten me that night, I don't remember. As soon as he had enough, he left me alone, and I allowed myself to sit on the ground. I lay against the bath, and the cold bathroom tiles caught my tears.
Now I understood why Cindy was afraid to admit it.
It becomes painfully clear what kind of hell Nell brought me to.
That night I became years older. And this turned out to be just the beginning of years of mental and physical abuse and neglect.

Wolf in sheep's clothing

The following morning I woke up on the cold bathroom floor. I looked around me and didn't know where I was.
I tried to sit down. My whole body ached, and suddenly I remembered again where I was and what had happened. Someone opened the bathroom door, and I saw Cindy appear in the doorway. I could see that she had been crying. 'Are you okay?'
I shrugged and tried to stand up.
'Come, let me help you.' Cindy grabbed my hands and helped me up until I was standing.
I felt woozy, and it felt like I could faint at any time.
I blinked a few times with my eyes to make the black marks disappear. Together we walked to the bedroom, where I lay down in my bed. Cindy tried to do well and pulled the blanket over me.
'I'm sorry, I am sorry.' She still avoided my eyes and started to cry.
'Leave me alone,' I said. I was angry and wanted to be left alone.
I turned myself around and felt a sharp pain shoot in my back.
I started to cry and tried to do this as quietly as possible. I didn't want Cindy to notice. I dozed a little until I heard something. With a jerk, I sat up straight in bed. I listened to howling, and it came out of the room where my little brother was sleeping.

I hurried directly to him.

Robbie stood up straight in the crib. His skinny legs crossed as logs from his oversized diaper.

Thick tears slid down his cheeks, and with a pout, he looked at me.

I climbed into the crib and pulled him on my lap. My entire body hurt very much, but this didn't interest me at that time. I made a promise to him. I would protect him with my own life.

Yolanda had heard the howling as she entered the room and saw us.

'Do you know how to change a diaper?' she asked.

I shook my head. Of course, I don't know how I have to do this. I was only five.

'Help your brother out of bed, and I will show you.'

I looked at Robbie, who was playing with his pacifier, then back to her.

'Come on, hurry up. I don't have time this whole day.' She looked impatiently at her watch. I gently lifted him out of the cot. He was pretty heavy for me, but I wanted to do it, so she didn't touch him.

'Lay him on the ground and pull out his pajamas. Then take off his diaper, and with these wet wipes, you wipe his buttocks and pecker clean. Do you understand me?'

'Yes, Ma'am,' I replied and did what she asked from me.

'You ensure that the diaper with the stickers' side is on the back, and you pull the front up and close the diaper with the stickers tight shut. Be careful that the comp is perfect and that your brother's pecker points down. Otherwise, he gets dirty and covered in pee. That is your problem, and you clean up the mess, have you understood this?'

Again I nodded obediently. I tried twenty times the diaper on and off to make sure that it was good. The stickers did not even stick anymore, and I had to use another diaper.

'Hi.' A light tinted boy of my age stands in the doorway.

He had black hair and wore an oversized pajama. His pants legs acted as socks on his feet.

'Hi,' I answered back.

'What's your name?' He asked, curious, and came closer.

'Elisa and you?'

'Jimmy.'

I smiled and raised my hand, 'Do you live here for a long time?'

'Since I was a baby. These people have adopted me because my mom didn't want me anymore. Just like your mother.'

These words caused me intense pain. I felt my tears coming up and was unable to stop them.

'Leave me alone. My mom comes to pick us up soon. That I know for sure, she promised me!' I shouted angrily.

He was terrified of my eruption.

'Sorry, I didn't want to make you upset.' Then he turned around and walked out of the room.

What a terrible kid! He was wrong about my mom. She had promised me when we said goodbye that she would come for us.

He knew nothing about her or us.

The arrival of the new children had spread like wildfire. It didn't take long until another child stuck her head around the corner of the door and curiously observed the new kids.

'Aren't you the new girl?' The girl looked at us extensively from head to toe. She wore specs that I think we're way too big for the frail girl. Half-long dark blonde hair, round face with Red Apple cheeks. A small and vulnerable girl to see. Because of the specs, she looked pretty smart.

I wiped away my tears.

'Hi, I'm Elisa. Who are you?'

'My name is Kim, Cindy is my sister, and we've been living here for six months.'

She seemed nicer than Jimmy, and we got to talk. We told each other about where we came from and about our parents, who we were missing.

The first weeks went by while I was waiting in vain for my mother.

I went to the new school for the first time. The school was at the end of the street where we lived. Primary school The Gandalf.

I had a lovely teacher, and it didn't take long before adapting to the new environment. My foster parents were more agreeable to me. They didn't hit me, and I was allowed to watch Sesame Street in the evening in the living room. Though I had been given the task to my brother's diaper, I had no problem.
I loved my little brother a lot, and there was nothing I would not do for him.
In the meantime, I had a close friendship with Cindy, Kim, and Jimmy. Jimmy was the favorite of our foster parents. He was allowed to join them at the table during dinner, while we got to eat in our room from a plate dished on the floor. They also were less severe to him. He played in the living room while we had to play in our bedrooms. Well, now I call this playing. But we didn't have many toys to play with, with only two Barbie dolls, a wooden dollhouse, and a few crayons.
Several weeks passed without anything having changed. Since I lived here, I peed every night in my bed, and when I woke up, I was soaking wet up to my knees.
The sheets and my pajamas were soggy and smelly.
I couldn't do anything about it, and I could not stop doing it. My foster parents found it odd and very annoying, so they decided to take me to the doctor.
Something was going on with me.
Yolanda sat in the waiting room, and I ran around looking for a Donald Duck magazine. Secretly I hoped that she would forget why we were here.

I would be ashamed if I went, and the doctor asks why I still peed in bed.

'Yolanda, I have a headache,' I sighed.

'Really, Elisa? You feel spontaneously bothered?' Yolanda didn't look up from the magazine she was reading.

'Well, then we must not forget to mention this in a moment to the doctor. If he asks, I give the answers, and you keep your mouth shut. Do you understand me?'

I nodded: 'Yes, Yolanda.'

The doctor came hurriedly walking in and apologized several times because we had to wait long. Yolanda told him, for which we had come and come up with a litany of lies.

Now and then, he wrote something on a paper, while his look wandered to his journal.

She lied almost every word, and he believed every one of them.

I sat on the edge of the chair to my knees. I pressed my tongue against my palate as hard as possible to stop them: the words stack to a big mountain in my mouth, which I wasn't allowed to say out loud. Yolanda would take the floor, and I had to keep my mouth shut.

Clicking sounds rolled through my mouth and escaped between my lips pressed together. Click. No, I'm not brutal and ungrateful. Click. No, I didn't have a fever last week. I do have headaches. Click, I didn't poop in the hallway; why does she tell such lies about me?

The doctor looked up from his journal, and dubiously looked at me with his pen in his mouth.
'Is everything okay with you?'
I nodded profusely.
'Do you see what I mean? This child is not normal.'
Once the doctor left the room to get a prescription, she squeezed my arm and growled viciously that I immediately had to stop with that nonsense.

'So Ma'am, give this to her daily twice with a glass of water, and then she will be fine.' The doctor returned with the medicine.
Grateful, she took the box, and we left. During our trip back home, it remained hushed in the car.
I looked at the cars that caught us. Maybe I saw my dad driving by. We went through the neighborhood where he and his wife rented an apartment. At every Red Opel that drove by, my heart made a jump of excitement, and I watched full of desire inside the car. Every time it turned out, it wasn't him. I leaned back, disappointed in the back seat.
'What's going on?' Yolanda observed me through the rearview mirror.
'I have abdominal pain,' I lied.
'When we get home, you go straight to bed. Take the pill first. Otherwise, you keep pissing in your bed like a baby, and that I will make you regret this time.'

As soon as we arrived home, she sent me straight to my room. I took a sigh of relief.
I wanted to know how Robbie was doing.
I would throw a glance in his room to see if he was okay. Peter paced back and forth through the living room, leaning on his stick.
'What's the matter with you, stupid Mongolian!' Yolanda screamed irritated.
'We get a visit.' Peter answered.
I caught the conversation while taking off my shoes in the hallway and was about to go to my room.
Who is coming, I wondered. Whoever it was, Peter turned out not so happy about it.
Yolanda entered the room moments later and gave me a pile of clothing in my hands. It was a new dress with tights for me and a sweater for Robbie.
'Change yours and your brother's clothes. Someone is here to see you.'
'Should I take my pill first?' I asked.
'Not now, you do that soon, but now you do what I ask you,' she snapped at me.
I dressed and took Robbie out of his room. He was happy to see me and greeted me cheerfully with his lovely smile.
'Come on. We're going to make you look beautiful. We received a visit. I believe that this is an essential visit because Peter is devastated.'

Robbie looked at me as if he wanted to say: what do you say to me? I have absolutely no idea.

Once I changed our clothes, I waited in suspense until she came.

It felt like every minute lasted at least one hour. Who would it be? Perhaps the lady who brought us here. I didn't know so many people.

Finally, it was time, the door opened. Yolanda came in and told us to join her in the living room.

As soon as the door opened, I saw my mother sitting on the couch.

'Mommy!' I ran to her and flew her around the neck. You see.

I knew it; she was here to take us home.

'Mama, I've missed you so much. Where were you? Can we go home?'

'O, my dear treasure of mine. I have missed you terribly.' She began to cry and held me tightly. 'But I'm not here to take you back home. I'm sorry, dear.'

'Why not?' I pushed her away from me and started crying. Tears were running down my face. I was angry and sad at the same time. Did she mean this? I didn't understand. Why? I felt my heart racing, and I gasped. It was the second time I felt heartbreaking. The first time was the day we said goodbye to her, and now she broke it again. Didn't she want us to live with her? Why did she come here?

'Why, mommy? What have we done wrong? You don't love us anymore?'
'No, sweetheart, that's not it. I love you, dearly. But I can't take care of your concerns. I do not have money to buy groceries, no money for new clothes or shoes. Yolanda and Peter take care of you, and I'm glad they want to do this.'
'I don't need new shoes! I want to go home!' I looked past the head of my mother to the people who are calling themselves our foster parents.
Shall I tell her what had happened the first night? I opened my mouth, but the words stuck. I doubted, what if Mama did not want to believe? Imagine that; they would surely beat me to death when I do that. I decided to keep my mouth and tried to enjoy my mother's presence.
In the meantime, I calmed down, but I was still full of questions.
The visit went by way too fast. Mama stood up and stroked with her hands over her dress.
'Mama, please don't go away. I beg you, take us home. I will do whatever you want; you have to give me just one slice of bread a day,' I begged her while the tears came forth again. I squeezed my little arms tightly around her waist and refused to let go of her. She had to stay with us. She should not go away. She could not leave us among these people.

Yolanda and Peter reassured mom that she could better leave directly, which was best for us.
I screamed and kicked wildly around me while Peter tried to loosen my arms from my mother's waist.
'Picture this. Elisa will calm down as soon as you leave the door. Departure now.'
My mother listened to him and ran as soon as she came loose, to the front door.
She looked back at us and cried.
'I come back soon again, dear ones. I promise.'
After these words, she pulled the door shut and left her children behind. I held on to her promise, but time would tell she didn't keep it.

After the visit, they send us directly back to our rooms.
The beautiful dress had to come off and got exchanged for the old and faded pajamas I typically wore at home.
I was overwhelmed by loneliness. Abandoned and rejected by my mother. Robbie looked dreamily while his legs dangled back and forth pressure.
I realized that I was not alone. I had my little brother close to me, and even though he could not speak yet, he was my very best friend. 'What if I told mom about how they treat us? Maybe she would take us back home?'
Robbie looked at me. She would not have believed us.
These people were just wolves in sheep's clothing.
No one sees what kind of beasts they are.

'Your mother is dead.'

I have been living there for one and a half years now.
My foster parents felt that it was time for more household chores when I was six. So every Saturday morning, I got a bucket with soap water in my hands and got summoned to the bathroom to brush and clean it. Once I finished, she came to verify that I had done my chores well.
I cleaned the whole bathroom, except that day I forgot about one small corner. Next to the washing machine was a little bit of dust.
'You told me that you were ready! What is this? Lazy tramp!'
The white spit was foaming layers of flakes on her lips, and her eyes spitfire.
Even before I opened my mouth, I felt a dull thud on my right eye. I fell on my shoulder against the washing machine and begged her not to be angry, and I didn't forget intentionally.
Yolanda didn't even listen to what I had to say. She pulled me by my hair to the bath and forced me over the edge to bend down.
I knew what to expect.
With the usual belt, she hit my back several times. So hard that I was afraid that she would break it. I screamed in pain. She picked up the bucket and poured the filthy

soap over me. It spread rapidly along the joints of the floor tiles.

'Clean it right now, and this time you make sure that you don't forget anything, do you understand?'

I was so scared that I had peed in my pants, but I didn't dare admit it because then she would be so mad at me again.

Once she had left the bathroom, I pulled down my underwear and washed it under the sink tap.

I stopped abruptly at every sound I heard.

I listened well if they came my way. After I cleaned my underwear well enough and wrung it out, I quickly pulled my pants back on, fell on my knees, and started to clean the floor.

My tears fell on the ground where I had just cleaned.

I was mad at myself.

How could I forget that corner? Yolanda was right; I was a lazy ass. God, I hated myself.

The moment I was sure that I didn't skip any spots, I called her again once I finished. Yolanda came checking and seemed this time satisfied with what she saw.

'Very well. Do you understand that you and only you are the cause of what has just happened? You must do your task properly,' she said calmly.

Her mouth corners were a little curled up as if she enjoyed what she did to me. She loved the power and control she had over us. The icy tone of her voice caused chills all over my body.

I nodded and ran towards my room.

The door of my brother's bedroom was open; he was sleeping in his crib.

Fortunately, he didn't notice anything that had happened. Of course, I was extra careful that I didn't forget anything the next time.

Besides the bathroom, also the bedrooms, the toilet, and the kitchen got added to my to-do list.

Every evening I had to wash the dishes.

In the beginning, Cindy had to help me with it. In the future, this would be Robbie's task in the house.

The next day I got up with muscle pain; the mirror was ruthless.

My one eye saw black and blue and did not open.

Yolanda came in and said: 'this morning, I bring you to school. You've fallen on the edge of your bed. Don't even think about telling the truth. No one would believe you if you told them what happened.'

I swallowed; it hurt because my throat felt as if a piece of sandpaper got stuck in it.

We walked to school together without speaking a word. The children are racing back and forth on the playground, and some teachers stood there to guard.

As soon as my teacher saw us, she came our way.

'What happened to you, sweetie?' she was startled.

She grabbed my head and turned it a little away from her. She reviewed the bump extensively.

'This looks painful. Have you already been to the doctor?'

She turned to Yolanda, equal in defense.

'She has fallen on her bed edge. She slipped when she wanted to climb in her bed, 'replied Yolanda.

'We found no need to bother the doctor that late. It wasn't necessary, right, Elisa? Tell the Miss what you told us that it didn't hurt that much. It looks worse than it is. Don't worry about her.' Yolanda wrapped her arm around me and squeezed dastardly in my shoulder.

I got tears in my eyes.

I clenched my jaws on each other.

It hurt. But I tried to hide my pain.

She experienced just more fun when I showed her my pain, which was the last thing I wanted to give her.

The Miss pulled up her shoulders and said, 'If you say so, but I will keep an eye on her. As soon as she is nauseous, I'll send her home.'

Around noon the headache got unbearable. Also, I had this feeling like I could throw up at any time. I told this to the teacher.

She said, 'Sweetie, go home and take your rest. Maybe you do have a slight concussion.'

I didn't like it to go home, but I could keep an eye on my little brother. I was scared to death that they would hurt him if I weren't around.

I was not there to protect him when I was at school. These thoughts gnawed each school day at me. As a result, I could not keep my focus well, and I ran behind in school results.

Yolanda was not happy to see that I got sent home.
I gave her the letter that the teacher had given to me. Advice to let a doctor check on my condition. She was worried about me and thought it was wise to have a doctor look at me, to exclude a concussion. But Yolanda didn't feel the same. She was busy painting her nails—a horrible red color.
'Go to bed and try to get some sleep. But make sure that you don't disturb me for the rest of the day.' She waved, with her hand, that I had to leave.
I hurried to my room and threw a quick look at Robbie. He was sleeping again.
I crawled in bed with my clothes still on and thought of my father. I haven't seen him since I lived there.
My father lived with his wife in Den Bosch.
He was married to her when he met my mother.
My parents got an affair, and one thing led to another. When my mother became pregnant, my dad didn't have any other option to go home and confess his misbehave. He left his wife to be with my mother.
Together they looked forward to the day that I would announce.
After my birth, it quickly went downhill with the relationship, and just after my second anniversary, they broke up.

My mother walked into someone else, the father of my brother. And my father went back to his ex-wife, who took him back into her life, despite everything. Everyone called her aunt Marie.
I called her over time, Madu. Madu is an old-fashioned name for mother.
It was hard for her to have a child around from the woman who had stolen her husband. But despite that, she has always taken good care of me. When I was with them, she took good care of me. The most important thing for me was that my father visited the arrangement after each appointment.
Then he picked me up on Friday afternoon and took me to the campsite in Breskens, "The Napoleon Hoeve."
There he had a mobile home next to the sea.
The campsite felt like my home. Here I felt safe and secure. Still, I carried a big secret with me, and I didn't share this with them.

The mobile home was eleven meters long and seven meters wide.
My father had built a large greenhouse. The caravan had old antique wooden furniture.
My father was a successful businessman. RTI transport was the name of his company. With a loan of six thousand dollars, he started his own moving company. One thing led to another, and the transport company was born, with which he earned several million.

At the campsite, in the summer was a lot to do. Especially for the children, there was an entertainment team—a large indoor swimming pool with a slide in the form of a lighthouse. In the game-room were all kinds of devices on which you could play video games.

Papa, Madu, and I often walked on the beach, looking for shark teeth that we gathered in a large glass jar.

My best friend came from Germany and was called Dominique. We created, built our secret hut, and often went swimming.

We were an inseparable team. Our parents became friends with each other, and as a result, we spent a lot of time together.

I enjoyed plenty of the time I spent with them. But unfortunately, there was a nasty flip side the moment we drove back to the foster family.

He played cassette tapes with music like Frank Sinatra, Dolly Parton, and Bob Carlisle in the car. That last one was my favorite. Especially the song Butterfly kisses.

As soon as that song played, I got tears in my eyes. Even though my father was sitting next to me in the car at that time, I missed him already.

He parked the car near the garden.

We walked hand in hand to the sliding doors in the garden.

Halfway through the grounds, he stopped, kissed me on my forehead, and whispered: 'I love you, little Princess, and be kind.'

I saw the tears in his eyes.

'I love you too, Daddy,' I whispered.

Please don't go away, don't leave me here, I thought.

I looked at my father, begging. I felt my tears burn.

On the outside, it didn't show, but inside I was torn apart by the grief.

I hated that moment most of all—moment of saying goodbye.

I fell asleep while crying. The farewell weighed most heavily. The lack of my parents, the circumstances in which we grew up.

A reflection of my image. I felt worthless, ugly, and stupid.

If even my mother didn't want me around her, how much was I worth?

No wonder my foster parents treated me like shit; I didn't earn better. I hated myself thoroughly and often thought about death. Sometimes this seemed to me this was the only way out, out of this hell. My mother did not have to be ashamed of her daughter, and my father would not feel sad about cheating.

Madu wouldn't be longer reminded of the slip that my father had committed and of the woman that had stolen her husband.

This kind of thought kept regularly going on in my little head.

But also questions such as: why was I born? Why does this all happen to me? Even though we were in a foster family with several children, I felt very lonely most of the time.

It didn't matter if the room was full. The loneliness and the emptiness layers always lurking and stroke at unexpected times. Before my father drove out of the street where I lived, he stopped once more to blow a hand kiss.

I jumped in the air to catch and to blow a kiss back.

Sometimes he forgot, and I returned to my room with an intense lousy feeling. Fortunately, there were also days that our foster parents left us alone.

Then they were too preoccupied with themselves.

These days we were able to recover from our life there.

Because no one kept an eye on us, on these days we played with each other in our rooms, we did or tried to play hide and seek in silence while we listened carefully. We take turns to keep guard. One of us was all the time at the door to hear if anyone arrived.

At every sound, we sat up straight like statues, and with a thudding heart, we waited for what was going to happen.

It's tough to find the right words to describe what this all did to us, what it does to a child being abused and neglected.

Even now, years later, the memories are still fresh of the terror.

The pain, the sadness, the loneliness, the despair, and the memories come back and change me into the same broken little girl.

Seven years old: one day afternoon, Robbie and I were sitting in my room to eat a sandwich. Yolanda came to our room, and in her hand, she held a brown envelope. Our names were on it.
The handwriting was familiar.
When she spread the envelope's contents on the table, we saw two small children—baby pictures of my brother and me.
'This has your mother left behind for you. I have to tell you something. Your mother is dead.'
I looked startled; This could not be true? We haven't seen her for a long time, but she couldn't be dead?
I burst into tears, and my little brother did not. He was too small to understand.
At that time, he was two years old.
I paused, not even asked for explanations. I could only cry and stare at the pictures where Mom held us in her arms. Yolanda picked up the images, and after a few minutes without saying anything, she left the room.
Before Yolanda closed the door, she turned back to us. The mean smile betrayed her; she created a sadistic pleasure in the sadness that I had. She was visibly proud of herself. The door fell behind her in the lock and left us behind. Reports and broken by grief. I ran while weeping

with my little brother to his cot and tried to read him a story. I failed; the words got stuck in my throat as razor-sharp knives.

I couldn't eat or sleep. I just kept crying and struggling with disbelief. Yolanda came to our room now and then to check what we were doing.

'Do you start whining and crying again, stupid child?'

I nodded and replied, violently sobbing: 'I miss my mom so much. Why is she dead? Was she sick? What happened?'

Her mocking laugh echoed through the room, and while evil smiling, she said that I had to stop whining like a baby. According to her, I had to be happy because now our mother no longer feels embarrassed for her moronic children.

Such a Witch! How dare she say something like that!

I was furious. I felt a primal force flare-up in my body. As a raging tornado, I started to shout, 'shut up!'

Her shrill laugh again echoed through the room. She turned her head to the door and stepped almost triumphantly out of the room. I could no longer control myself. I jumped on her back and grabbed her ponytail with both of my hands. I hated her intensely, and I didn't know what kind of punishment I would get; for all I care, they would beat me to death. It was worth it.

Her hysterical screech had reached the living room and made sure that Peter rushed into our room. In my opinion, he was terrified by what he saw because it took a while before he responded.

He saw me on the back of his wife and tried to loosen my hands from her ponytail.

He grabbed my neck and squeezed heavily, handed in my neck muscle. I kept the hair between my fingers and was determined to leave a big bald spot on the head from that evil bitch.

Forty-three hits with the walking stick were my punishment. Each time it landed on my back, I shouted out loud that it didn't hurt, and I hated them. After the last time, they closed the door behind them with a loud bang. The window above the door was shaking because of that. It didn't matter how many times they beat me, as long as they kept their hands off my little brother.

Now our mother was dead, I took the responsibility, the education and care of my little brother even more seriously.

We played with imaginary cars, I made up stories about Princes and Knights to tell him, and we played hide and seek in the bedroom.

That was so cute.

Then he hid under the bed, and as soon as I started to search, I saw two mini-foot protrudes under the crib.

He hides himself every time in the same place.

I was looking desperate for the master of hiding.

I act like I could not find him and heard loud giggles come from under the bed where he hid.

The smile on his face made every horrible thing just right. He had a smile of inestimable value. It worked contagious because it didn't matter how miserable I felt; he always made me feel cheerful.
The days lasted long. We sat in our room after school and tried to invent games for which we needed no toys.

I laid down and looked through the window.
I saw a blackbird on the railing of the Canal. He jiggled excitedly from left to right, and he held between his beaks a spring of clamp. I was wondering whether the bird had baby birds. Would he take good care of them and feed them well?
I wanted to change into a bird, and then I would fly directly away from this hell, to my father and Madu.
I wanted to be free. But it was only a dream, a dream that sat locked behind the window of my bedroom. It seemed like an impossible task to escape from here. My foster parents held everything locked down, and once in a while, they check on us to see if we behave ourselves.
One day Yolanda was very busy in the house. She even had barely time to keep an eye on us. We all could hear what been said in the living room.
'Lazy bastard, can you help me? That man is on the pavement. What she thinks of us as she sees this mess.'
'Oh, don't worry, woman. She comes to cut the hair of the children. We will vacuum later.'

'She needs to do something about their hair. I'm tired of combing it every time. What do you think, curtail?'
Peter nodded in agreement and looked further at the tennis match that was on television.

The hairdresser arrived in the evening. We have to take turns in the dining room chair, which stood in the kitchen. Yolanda said to the young lady with scissors that she had to cut my long hair into a short boy's hairstyle. The woman looked down at my hair and asked Yolanda if she was sure about that.
'I think it will be ashamed of her beautiful long hair, though. I think you're going to regret it,' she told Yolanda.
'Listen, I'm getting sick and tired of the tangles in their hair. I have better things to do than to waste an eternity combing the hairs of those children.'
My hair never got cut, so once the hairdresser finished, I didn't know where my long hair went; it was all gone.
'I want my hair back!' I screamed in panic. I was angry.
I looked like a boy and knew that for sure because even Yolanda started to laugh when she saw me. I hated her.
I ran upset back to my room, where the girls were waiting until their turn.
'Jesus, you look ridiculous!' shouted Kim.
'Shut your mouth. I don't need to feel mocked at one more time.'

Once all the children had their haircut, the hairdresser left again.

At the moment she pulled the door behind her, Yolanda stormed into our room. She grabbed me by my short hair and sold me a pair of firm smacks.

'Goddamn, I hate you, evil child. You are disgusting.'

'Peter, come here!'

Peter came into the room. 'What's going on?'

'That evil child makes a fool out of me in front of the hairdresser. I got fed up with it, and you must now teach her a lesson. You let me usually do it, but do it this time yourself.'

'Come with me and act normal. Send the kids to bed, so we can finally eat dinner.' Peter complained.

While Yolanda leaves the room, Peter begins to shout at me. Louder and louder, until he had a wild look in his eyes.

He grabbed me by my arm and pulled me to the living room.

'Tell your mother that you're sorry.'

I kept silent.

'Say you're sorry.'

'No, I didn't do anything wrong, so I am not going to say 'I'm sorry,' and besides that, she's not my mother!'

I got a bang against my head.

'You apologize right now; say you're sorry!'

I didn't have any chance. Because my head hurt terribly, and I didn't want more pain.

'I'm sorry, mama.'
'And now you tell her that you love her.'
I looked at him and doubted. I immediately got a nasty taste in my mouth as soon as I uttered those words.
'I love you, mama.'
'Give her a hug.'
I sighed deeply; I didn't want to do that.
'Why?' I asked and grimaced.
'Hurry up. Otherwise, I smack your head again,' threatened Peter. Yolanda stood with a grim face looking the other way, with her arms folded.
'Damn woman, well hug that child back. Then you can finally start cooking.'
With great reluctance, I put my arms around her for a second, and I ran back to my room with a queasy feeling. That came after saying the words, 'I love you.'

I was disgusted by myself, and I jumped under the shower to wash her skin cells off of me. I cherished intense hatred for them. So much that I even thought about killing them. But how could I do that?
I was only a child.
In the week, Robbie suddenly got sick. He got a high fever and could not hold anything inside.
Every time I went with him up and down to the toilet, he hung above the toilet bowl and threw up what he had eaten that day. Every five minutes, he needed a new diaper and kept vomiting.

I felt hopeless. Hesitantly I knocked on the door of the living room.

'What do you need?' Peter sat on the couch and was watching television.

'Robbie is sick, and I don't know what to do.'

Peter seemed annoyed; he sat in the middle of a tennis tournament that aired on the NPO, the local broadcast.

'How should I know? Figure it out yourself. Explain to Robbie to lay down in bed, and if he throws up, well, you know what to do, clean it!'

I shut the door behind me.

Peter is such a jerk. He didn't even help me with this.

Yes, my vocabulary expanded with time. It was in this home a daily routine that Yolanda scolded anyone who got in her way. The most dreadful imprecations flew around, along with the blobs of spit that came out of her mouth. Here we were allowed to enjoy it, and I would bet our neighbors as well, as those two started a fight with each other. Figural speaking, because as far as I know, they never literally attacked each other.

For that, they used us.

After I had washed and had given Robbie a few sips of water, he finally fell asleep. Yolanda came rushing into our room later in the evening.

'Who used the bathroom?'

Cindy and Kim looked at each other and said in unison that it wasn't them. Yolanda turned to me, and I could tell from the look on her face, something was very wrong.

I took the blame on myself because I already had a suspect where this was going. She asked me to follow her to the toilet, and I saw why she got so angry.

My little brother had accidentally vomited beside the toilet bowl.

Heavy-handed, she pushed me against the ground with the communication to clean as soon as possible.

With a roll of toilet paper, I started to clean. The vomit was everywhere. On the pot, against the walls. Even against the door frame and the door. I used a whole roll of toilet paper to clean it.

Once I cleaned it, I threw all the used toilet paper in the toilet and pulled it through. The water just kept rising.

I tried with my hand to push the prop further, but that did not help one bit. The water had already reached the edge and flowed about the tiles in the Hall. I had no idea what I had to do and screamed for help.

As soon as my foster parents saw what was going on, they were going ballistic. Peter cared about the flood, while Yolanda had to address me. They had the opinion that I had done it on purpose, and I would pay for it.

I protested vehemently, but I realized that this doesn't make any sense. Therefore, I ran out of myself to the bath, pulled my Nightshirt off, and bow in anticipation over the edge.

The belt was not within easy reach, so she hit me several times with a broom handle. It wasn't a piercing pain as with the belt, but it still was excruciating. I felt how the shank with a dull thud came down on my back, on the places where Peter had earlier hit me with his stick. With my eyes and mouth pinched, I collected the beating. I tried to think of the campsite, my father, and Madu.
The taste of blood brought me back to reality. I bite on my tongue.
Afterward, I returned, limping back to the bedroom. Robbie stood crying in the doorway of his room.
He woke up and heard everything that had happened.
'Darling, go back to bed. You're sick.'
I didn't find the strength to bring him to his bed, so I asked him to do it by himself. Luckily he obeyed me and did what I asked.
The other children in the family were increasingly hiding behind me. They knew I would take the blame on me for them.
After all, I was the oldest of the foster children and had a great sense of responsibility as a big sister.

Listen or Die

Our family expanded with the arrival of a new child. Mees. A little boy of one year old, he laughed all day.
He and Robbie became best friends over the years.
They slept together in the room that they had to share with Jimmy. Because Mees still wore a diaper, he also needed someone to change them for him. Since I already have my little brother, Cindy got this responsibility.
She was not happy about it. Each time it was a lot of complaining once Yolanda had turned her back. From the time she had to do that, it changed her into a conniving maid.
Well, she was already not a sweetie, but since that time, she acted more like a bitch to me. She kept kissing ass all day long from our foster mother, and her backstabbing behavior got rewarded. She and Jimmy got allowed to play in the living room, and there was no need to change diapers anymore, and they drank cozy tea at the kitchen table. She was meaner than ever before, even in front of her sister.
When I came out of school one day, I saw her hiding behind Yolanda.
She looked at me in a certain way, so I quickly realized that something was going on. Yolanda invited me to follow her to our bedroom.
Cindy turned out to have betrayed me.

She had told Yolanda where I hide my breakfast every morning because I simply can't swallow it in the morning.
But the rule was: you finish what's on your plate or get hit by one of them.
To avoid this, I try to hide my breakfast in a bag under my bed.
Yolanda took out the bag and kept it in front of my nose.
You could see mold through the plastic bag.
'What's this?' she asked me.
'I don't know,' I lied.
Her mouth left, and I knew that she caught me. Because I was expecting a smack, I automatically popped down. But she didn't hit me. However, she did something I didn't expect at all.
She grabbed my hand and pulled me to the living room. There she picked up the high chair from Mees.
'Sit down,' she said.
I was confused. Could Yolanda mean that for real?
I would never fit in; it was a chair for babies.
'Come on,' she snapped at me.
I pushed my legs through the seat and sat down. It was tight.
She put the pouch open and said: 'you are going to eat it all, and you remain in this seat until the bag is empty.'
I started to cry and begged her not to do this.
The bread was moldy, and I could not eat it. I would get sick. No, much worse, I could die.

But she held firm. I had to empty the pouch anyway.

Meanwhile, Cindy got instructed to bring everyone to the living room, where I sat in the seat. Also, my little brother had to watch how I had to eat moldy bread. Yolanda began to sing:'hump...'
She urged the rest to join. They obeyed and started singing along instantly.
Including my brother, and as if that wasn't enough, they laughed at me because of the child seat. Still, I dared not to touch the bread. Yolanda got wild. She picked up a piece of bread from the bag and popped it in my mouth.
I felt her fingers deep in my throat. I started to gag.
My mouth filled with vomit and mingled with the bread.
'Don't you even dare to spit it out! I'll let you eat all of it.'
It was horrible! Worst of all was not that I had to eat moldy bread, also not that I had to sit in a highchair.
But the worst thing I found was that my little brother was about to look at his big sister and sing with them.
That broke my heart.
I could not blame Robbie; he was so young, vulnerable, and still unaware of the indoctrination. If he didn't do what he got told to do, Yolanda would hit him.
It took four hours before I ate it all.
I had eaten all the pieces of bread, as she demanded.
I rather got hit with a belt than to get so humiliated in front of my blood brother.

Nauseous and broken, I left myself sliding in bed and pulled the blanket over my head as far as possible.

That evening I spit everything out of my body.

I kept vomiting for hours. I was relieved when nothing more came out, and I finally could fall asleep. That was the only thing I desired. That night I wanted to dream about running away.

While I listened to the rain which clattered against the window, I figured an escape plan to carry out.

What I didn't know was that my plan would quickly come in handy.

Run for your life!

Robbie and I were in the kitchen.
My job was doing dishes that afternoon, and Peter thought that the time had come that my little brother was old enough to help me. Such a young child, you can't expect it to do chores and not from my little brother, who was so clumsy already.
It didn't last an eternity before a plate fell and broke. The shards spread layers all over the kitchen floor.
Peter jumped up from his chair and came into the kitchen. 'Goddamn, stupid! Be careful and watch out if you're doing something!'

He raised his hand and beat my little brother with a munch against the ground. Robbie began to cry. I popped in a panic and looked around me. The only thing within easy reach was his walking stick.
The stick hung on the chair near the sink. It was a wooden cane with a round handle. I hesitated for a second, hooked the handle to Peter's ankle, and pulled it with all my strength. With a hard sound, he fell to the ground.
I grabbed my little brother at his hand and ran as hard as I could with him, out of the door. I heard Peter shouting that he would kill me.
Adrenaline spouted through every fiber of my body: a euphoric feeling, the feeling of victory. On socks, we ran

down the street towards the shopping center behind our home. A good friend of my father, whose name was Hank, had his dry cleaning. He would help us.
But when I got there, the mall was closed. It was Sunday, and I had completely forgotten about this.
My little brother was out of breath.
I lifted him on my back and ran through the bushes and flowerbeds to find a place where we could rest. I look back to see if nobody follows us.
A classmate at school in the circle told us that she had built a cabin with her brothers.
It had to be there somewhere in the neighborhood. A little further away, I found the cabin. I put my little brother down and pulled my jersey out to keep him warm. It started to cool down outside, and he felt cold.
I sat down close to him and kept waiting, in case our foster parents found us. It was dark, and the stars were visible. High in the sky seemed a star brighter than the rest. I figured out that this was the star of our mom.
'Look, Robbie, there is mama's star.'
I asked God: 'Dear Lord, can you protect us tonight and make sure that we do not get found.' Then I fell asleep with my arms around Robbie.
The next morning I woke up to the sound of school-age children. Then I found out that the cabin built by the girl was right behind our school. My little brother woke up and started crying. He was hungry and needed a clean diaper.

'Keep quiet. I'm going to look for food and will also bring a new diaper. But you can't leave the cabin, okay?'
I asked him to pinky swear before I went on the road.
I looked skittish around me. I was scared to death that they would recognize me or could see that I ran away. No one seemed to notice the little girl on her socks.
I walked through the shopping mall looking for the dry cleaning of Uncle Hank. The shop turned out to be close. There hung a piece of paper on the door that read: "CLOSED for remodeling."
I would try again later and run towards the supermarket. I picked up a bag of bread rolls at the grocery store and hid a few diapers under my t-shirt, which I had taken from a pack after I secretly had ripped it open. My heart raced at that time. I was afraid of getting caught.
From the moment I passed the cashier, I ran until I was outside the shopping center.
Once outside, I put it on the run back to the cabin, where my brother was waiting for me. We ate together, and then I changed his diaper.
I found out that I had forgotten the wipes. I searched around me for clean leaves and cleaned Robbie's legs.
It was not ideal, but in the end, I managed to get him clean. Three nights we slept in the cabin under the stars. Several times a day, I walked to the mall for bread, milk, and diapers to steal.

I'm still impressed that they didn't catch me at that time. The fourth day it went wrong. The girl, who had built the cabin, came along with another girl to play there.
'What are you doing here? Your parents told the miss you were sick.'
'They are not my parents, and I'm not sick,' I called indignantly. 'I've run away, and I am never going back.'
The girls looked frightened at each other.
'Why not?' now asked the other girl.
'Because they abuse us and are quite mean to us, and I'll never go back.'
I got the idea that they didn't believe me.
'Promise me that you don't tell a soul that we are hiding here!' They swore to keep both their mouths shut, but I had a suspicious feeling about it.
My feeling proved correct. Half an hour later, my foster parents came together with the girl's parents towards the cabin.

'We have been looking for you, baby. We've been so damn worried, don't you ever run away from home.' Yolanda kneels for me and strokes her hand, the hair for my eyes. These were not combed in four days and were full of tangles.
'I ran away,' I protested loudly. 'You're a bad mother, and I hate you!'
The girl's parents were shocked by my response.
'Help me,' I begged them.

But Yolanda told them. 'The poor child has a mental illness. She is a pathological liar, and she sees no difference between the truth and her fantasies. She has medications for it, and here you can notice that she didn't take these for a few days.' The parents nodded in agreement and said it was good that their daughter informed them.
'They lie! I'm not crazy,' I shouted.
How could they believe them? I couldn't understand it. But there was no option left but to go home. I took my little brother by the hand and kept my eyes on my foster parents. Once we arrived home, the bath got filled by Yolanda.
'Take your clothes off and sit in the bath,' she snapped.

I pulled my socks last. They looked muddy, and one has a hole at the height of my big toe. When I wanted to let down my foot gently in the bath, Yolanda lifted me and threw me into the tub. The water was boiling and burned my skin. I screamed and tried to climb out of the bath. She pushed me back. 'You stay in the bath, you dirty beast. You smell horrible and need to get clean.'
She scrubbed with a brush, heavy-handed my body. While she did this, she spoke to me in a disparaging tone.
'You little bitch, let this be a lesson to you. We will always find you. Do you think you are smart? You are nothing more than a piece of shit, do you hear me?' She

had polished so hard that burns appeared on my skin. While she was drying me, she noticed them, and she ran away without saying anything. She came back into the bathroom with a bottle in her hands.

'This must be well disinfected,' Yolanda said.

She picked up a cotton ball and poured some water from the bottle on it.

Then she printed the cotton ball on the patches while she held me tightly with her other hand.

The bottle turned out to contain alcohol. I screamed out loud. That hurt so much! It stung terribly.

Rather dead than alive

'Stand still, stupid child.' Yolanda grabbed me tighter and squeezed hard in my upper arm.
'This hurts,' I whimpered.
'I don't care. You keep silent. Otherwise, I will make you pay for it.'
I shook my head.
'I thought so,' she said with a dirty grin on her face.
I wanted to kill her, but the power was missing. I was exhausted. Preferably I crawled under my blanket to fall asleep.
But that had to wait. Yolanda had another job for me in mind.
'So, now you can put your little brother in the bath. I'm tired and going to lay down in bed.' She turned, and I breathed a sigh of relief. Even though I was so tired, taking care of my little brother was never a problem for me. I left the bath drain and filled it with warm water. I felt with my wrist if the temperature was right. I had read about this in a magazine for expecting parents at school that I found in the teacher's room.
Still, a little bit of cold water was needed, and then it was perfect. My little brother was playing on the ground in his room. He looked vulnerable. I wondered what went through his little mind.

'Robbie, come with me to…'

Robbie stopped playing and turned towards me. 'Away?'
'No, sweetie, we're going to take a shower. We're not going away, 'I replied. He began to cry. I was shocked; he had more inherited than I initially thought. 'I'm sorry,' I said and gave him a hearty hug. While I hugged him, also tears came to me.
'I promise you I will always protect you,' I whispered in his ear.
'Come; first, you have to take a bath, and then I read a little story for you, okay?' He nodded. Together we walked to the bathroom, and the water had cooled down too much. Once the water was back at the right temperature, Robbie entered the bath. He had stopped crying but seemed with his thoughts somewhere else.
I filled a cup with the warm bath water and poured it over his head and back gradually. I could notice that this relaxed him.
I managed to lift him out of the bath with great difficulty and pulled him into his pajamas. 'Vroom, Vroom.'

Robbie is from one car to the other in his blue pajamas, 'Vroom'
'Such beautiful cars! They must be very tired of such a long drive. Jump on my back, and then I bring you quickly to bed.'
That was not so smart of me. Because of the lack of a good night's sleep, I wobbled when he climbed on my back and dropped through my knees.

'Maybe it's better if you walk by yourself to your room.' We took place in his crib, and I read him a piece from the book 'Cinderella' It didn't take long until he fell asleep. I decided that night to stay with him and also fell into a deep sleep.

The next morning I was awakened by Jimmy. 'Wake up. Hurry up, quickly to your room.'

I was startled awake and asked what's going on. 'You are not supposed to sleep here if mom and dad see this; they are going to hurt you again.'

'I'm going already.' I climbed out of bed. Robbie slept quietly through.

I opened the door of the room and looked through a crack to check if it was clear. It appeared that our foster parents were not awake yet.

I opened the door a little further and took a step outside the room.

At the same time, the living room door opens, and Peter steps outside.

'What are you doing out of bed, and what are you doing there with the boys?' He bellowed with a solemn voice.

I freaked out and stammered:

'Uh, nothing. I thought I heard someone cry and wanted to see if I could do anything so that you don't have to get out of bed.'

'Hm,' he grumbled. 'Go back to your room.'

I ran as soon as I could back to my room. The girls gobbled as quickly as I came in.

'Where were you?' They asked.
'Runaway.' I took out my nonchalant shrug.
'You have no idea how angry they were. Mom and dad have searched very near. Papa kept yelling that he would kill you as soon as he found you.'

'I'm sorry that I didn't take you with me too. But I didn't think of this at that time. Peter hit Robbie. I had to protect my brother.'
I felt guilty. The other children were in the same shitty situation as I was. We were all victims of these sick people who celebrated their frustrations on innocent children.
Small children were unable to defend themselves against injustice.

Many years later, while I'm writing my story down, I relived all of it again.
I will try to remember the details and find the right words to describe how it felt what they were doing to us.
They made us not only physically broken but also mentally.
That was our daily routine.
According to them, I was stupid, ugly, dumb, retarded, moron, and not worth living. My mother couldn't love me or want me around. And we were the cause of her death; she could no longer live with the idea that she had put such mentally disabled children on this planet.

My school results got worse every semester. I couldn't focus properly on the lesson and failed big time in the semester.

During the nights I woke up and kept staring at the ceiling, those broken nights began now to take their toll on me. For this reason, I had to leave the Gandalf school, with the advice to transfer me to the Titus Brandsma School.

A school for maladjusted children and children who needed more support in learning. This school was opposite the house of my aunt Francis. She was the sister of my father. Also, my little brother came as soon as he turned five years old to this school. Together we drove to school each morning with a taxi van, which picked up other children at their home.

It soon became apparent that I had no trouble with learning. The subject matter was relatively too easy, and effortlessly I got through it. On some subjects, I ran three levels ahead.

In the long term, the teachers told me that I could sit down in the library while the other kids in my class had to follow the lessons. In a classroom converted to a school library, my relationship with books grew. There was a brown leather armchair, which sat very comfortably. I crawled in it, and I got carried away by the stories that I was reading. I loved that. The harsh reality was at those times a far-from my-bed show.

I devoured book after book; the thicker they were, the more I loved to read them.

Besides these moments, my school-time wasn't fun at all. The bullying began. Every day I was bullied, called names, harassed, and sometimes beaten up by my class kids. In retrospect, they did this because they felt that I was the favorite of the teacher. The others had to stay in the classroom while I often was allowed to do something else, such as reading or water the plants.

The bullying and the home situation made me a small, scared, and insecure girl.

I kept my opinion for myself rather than to face the confrontation. Always look for the confirmation of another: poor self-image, low self-esteem. Everyone ran over me. I was too scared to do anything in return. Now I'm a grown woman and mother of three children. But deep down inside me is still the little girl's presence. Even though I now dare to give my opinion and I stand up for myself. The fear of not being good enough and getting abandoned played an essential role in my life for years.

Cake & plaster

1 May 1994, it was my ninth birthday.
That morning I was awakened with the announcement that they had a surprise for me. A suspicious feeling came to me.
What were they up to this time? Granted, they had not beaten me for quite some while, and I had to do fewer tasks. Why they were so lovely to me, I had no idea. But I didn't mind. All the children were neatly dressed, and after breakfast, we hit the road. The journey took a long time.
We kept ourselves busy with games like
'I see, I see what you don't see.'
In the clouds, we looked for figures, and we sang songs.

My heart made a jump from joy at the time that the lighthouse emerged. I screamed out: 'We're going to the campsite!' Yolanda looked at me and smiled. Even as she smiled in a friendly way, I still got the chills from her. Yolanda was a beautiful woman to see, but her appearance was terrible. Dark like she hid the devil, hoping that no one else would see it, would notice what her true identity was. We approached the campsite, and behind the long line of trees, I saw my father and I started to cry.
I had missed him so damn much. Once the car stopped, I jumped out of the car and flew into his arms.

'Hey girl, happy birthday! Do you like your surprise?'
'Yes, of course.' I felt so happy at that moment.
That was the best surprise of my life.
The children looked their eyes out at the campsite. They saw the pool, the lighthouse slide, the playgrounds, and tennis courts.
I led them over the paths along with the caravans and tents towards our mobile home. I thought that was a fantastic sound—the gritting and crunching sound of the shells under my feet.

'Oh, you need to look here,' called Kim. And she pointed to the ducklings that swam in the ditch—a mother-and father duck with seven small chickens.
'How sweet!' We called in unison.
Then I saw my Madu in the doorway waiting for us.
I ran towards her and hugged her. 'Mama, I've missed you so much.'
She cuddled me a little firmer and whispered in my ear:
'I missed you too, sweetheart.'
'Look, guys, this is our mobile home, and behind is my bedroom. Do you want to see it?' Everyone nodded in agreement and followed me to my room.
My room had Barbie wallpaper and pink curtains hanging in front of the windows.
I jumped on my bed and helped my little brother on it. He looked so cute that day, with his bowtie and in a neat

shirt. That day was fantastic, and I forgot all about the misery.
I was with my parents with my little brother, and everyone was happy and loving that day. The time had come that we all had to repeat farewell and had to return home. I cried during the whole trip.

Another year went by.
The days crawled over as lethargic elderly snails. Every day was the same as the day before. At half-past seven, we had to wake up. It was pretty cold each morning in the room, and the heating was not allowed to go on because it cost too much money. Hastily we put on our clothes, which Yolanda had given us the night before. Once we finished, it was time for breakfast. Plastic covers were used as plates and placed for us on the ground. Our breakfast was a sandwich with sticky fruit sprinkles. The combination of that sandwich and the filthy lukewarm milk, which often had a weird aftertaste, made me skip breakfast for years. But I had to eat it anyway; the alternative was getting beaten up because they called me ungrateful, and I wanted no repeat of that. So I ate all of it. When the taxi arrived, we had to make sure we were outside as soon as possible. It even happened that I forgot my shoes before I ran out. I was so afraid of their reaction if they thought that we had lingered and gave the kids at school one reason more to make fun of me.

I used to sit next to the window on the school bus. I was always daydreaming on the way to school. What it would be like to be mature. With my nose pressed against the window, I dreamed about a private cottage, a sweet man, maybe even becoming a mother.

I knew very well that the way they treated us was wrong, so I promised myself that I would do differently with my child, keep her safe, feel loved, comfort her if she was in pain, and never abuse her.

These thoughts kept me busy throughout the journey until the bus driver disturbed my dream, announced that we had arrived at school. With a deep sigh, I stood up and stepped out of the bus.

We were not allowed to play outside when we reached our home after school. Only if there was a birthday and they had to take pictures. You can imagine how happy we were on those days, and they set up an old tent. Then we got old clothes, and we could dress up. We played the game father and mother to heart's content. All other days we spend in our bedrooms, locked up. There were no toys to entertain us. So I developed my creative side.

I played imaginary with two Barbie dolls. From weekly magazines, I cut images with good food on them.

No advertisement about pasta, vegetables, or meat did escape to my greedy cut arts.

I fold it up as neat as possible, and I put it in my pocket to take home.

I played as if I was a top chef and went diligently to work in my imaginary kitchen. Out of the sky, I picked up the pans from one of the kitchen cabinets. The stove turned on, and soon, the water ran through our mouths. Around six o'clock, we got a warm meal of the day. It was only a small portion. A sick chicken ate more than what we got.

We got our food served as if we were animals: a plate on the ground.

Our foster parents always ate at the kitchen table in the living room. One of us had the luck and the honor of being present. Once back in the room, she or he told in scents and colors what was on the menu and how good it tasted. Of course, everyone saw green with envy.

The consequence was there was jealousy amongst the children. I tried to keep myself out of the fights. But I can't deny that I felt no jealousy.

My favorite moment was right before bedtime. Then I figured out what I wanted to dream about that night and fell asleep.

And I dreamed of the most beautiful things in life. I was the mother of all the children in the world that had no mom or dad to take care of them. I bathed them, cooked for them, comforted the children as they had pain, read stories to them before bedtime, and cuddled them quite often. In the morning, I could still remember exactly where my dream stopped, and I picked up where I left at night, the time I crawled into the sleeping bag, which had to act as a blanket. Of course, there were also regular quiet days. If we kept quiet and calm, we had peace.

It almost looked like they had forgotten about us. So it happened a few times that we had been so quiet that our foster parents forgot to bring us dinner in the evening, no warm meal. We crawled into our bed with an empty stomach as soon as it got darker.

In the evening, we all were so quiet that you could hear a pin drop. But on those days, the only sound that you heard was of our rumbling stomachs.

The summer holiday from '95 started.

But that wasn't a reason to feel happy. The days lasted just longer now. We didn't go to school, and we only could sit in our room with hardly any toys. But as soon as the taxi approached our Street, I saw to my delight the tent outside. Cindy and Kim walked around on high heels in oversized dresses.

Jimmy wore an oversized brown coat and had a hat on. Yolanda and Peter sat in the front yard to enjoy the sun. It was all summer, the sun was shining, and all the flowers were in bloom. The grass was full of daisies, from which I made a beautiful necklace. We played father and mother, hide and seek, tag, and sunbathing in the grass. In the first weeks of the holiday, we had such beautiful weather. We were allowed to play outside every day.

In the afternoon, tea or lemonade syrup got served in the tent, and in the evening, we were allowed to shower at sunset.

That was like heaven to us. We didn't previously feel this happy. No one got beaten up; our foster parents were less stressed and left us alone.

The last two weeks of the holiday went in, and all of the children got picked up by the parents. Only Jimmy stayed behind in the family. I also got picked up by my father. I was happy to see him again. My little brother went from this summer, staying with a single woman.

She was a warm and loving woman. She had already experienced enough in life, and for personal reasons, she had opened her heart for children looking for a place in someone's heart. Her name was Ineke. A slim woman with brown curly hair.

'Dad, good to see you. Are we going again to the campsite? And where is mama?'

I fired some questions at him. I babbled that I forgot to take a breath. O, I missed him so much.

'Hey, little girl.' He lifted me and took me in his arms. 'Of course, we go camping, and Madu is already there. She is waiting for you.'

In his arms, I felt secure with the best rates guaranteed.

We went on our way. The journey took a long time for me, but I didn't mind this. I loved to go on trips together with my dad. Then we sang songs, watched the trucks on the road, and did the game 'who counts most pheasants?'

In the car was a standard packet of Stimorol chewing gum, and as soon as we were in Belgium, we stopped for French fries with mayonnaise. 'Keep a place free for dinner, 'repeated my father every time. Mama always had dinner ready when we arrived. Once we arrived, we began at the last ritual. This last part took care of the final standings of the ride.
Who saw the lighthouse this time as first?
I still don't know why, but my heart rate went up at that time. I hung out with my chin on the dashboard and searched in the distance for the lighthouse. And then there was that moment, the lighthouse.
'I see him!' I screamed.
My father sighed overly deep and then said: 'Well, now you beat me again. I will never win from you.'
'Well, dad, there is only one who is the best, and you are not good enough to beat me.' I stuck up my nose and had to laugh.
'The next time you will win,' I reassure him. My dad laughed and stroked his hand over my head. I knew very well that he let me win every time, but I didn't tell him that.

Madu was as always in the kitchen as soon as we came in. It smells delicious. 'Mother, how nice to see you again.
How are you?' I asked while I hugged her.

'Good sweetheart, and how are you? Doing well in school?'
'Yes, very well,' I lied. That was always my answer when someone asked how I was doing. Always good. I dared not to tell my parents. I was afraid that they wouldn't believe me.
No one did that. But it was as always at each visit on the tip of my tongue.
I wanted to tell them what they did to us, about the beatings with the brown belt, locking us up in the rooms, and how little we got to eat. I doubted, would I tell them this time? Maybe he took Robbie and me away from that awful place if he knew what kind of horrible people they were. I looked at my father, who sat in his chair in front of the TV. Then to madu, who was stirring into the pots and pan. No, maybe some other time. I didn't want to think about it now, and I was finally with my dad. It was a holiday, and as always, it was mostly cozy.

I walked to my father and crawled on his lap. We continued to sit like this until Mom called us that dinner was ready.
That day there were boiled potatoes with cauliflower and lamb chops on the menu. That was my favorite food. Even though it was in the middle of the summer, you just made my day with this meal. Mom knew this very well, and she looked at me with a smile.
I smiled back and whispered gratefully: 'thank you.'

The first bite was the best one.

I enjoyed a lot of my mother's cooking skills, and my father did too. The gravy pearls hung from his chin. I secretly chuckled and took another large bite.

'It's delicious, honey,' he muttered with his mouth still full.

'Don't talk with your mouth full,' corrected Mom every time and shook her head.

'Is Dominique here too?' I asked now with my mouth still full.

'I think so,' replied my father. 'You can take a look, but after dinner is done.' The table was not clean, or I sprinted outside.

'Dominique?'

I stood at the gate in front of their caravan. 'Dominique, are you there?'

I yelled one more time. I saw someone sliding a small piece of the curtain aside. It was Dominique, and as soon as he saw me, he motioned for me to wait there. The door flew open, and Dominique came out and shouted: 'Elisa, how are you?'

'Good? Wanna come and play?' I asked, begging, and folded my hands in prayer mode.

'Of course,' he said and began to laugh.

We ran behind each other on the tarmac road along the ditch. We laughed and shrieked it out. My father stood in the garden and called us to him.

'Do you guys want ice cream?'
What kind of question is that? Of course, we want it. Ice cream is the best thing for a child in the summer, right?
A little later, we sat down on the stairs from the caravan. I looked at Dominique; he was enjoying his Magnum ice cream.

'Can you keep a secret?'
Dominique looked surprised.
'The people who take care of me are evil. They beat the other children and me, and we have to stay in our room. But you can't tell this to anyone else, though. They won't believe you anyway. But I just want someone to know, and it's so hard to keep it to myself.'
His beautiful blue eyes looked at me in disbelief and sincere condolences too.
He put his arm around me and gently gave a kiss on my cheek. 'Friends forever.'
I knew my secret would be safe with him.
It was a fantastic week, which flew by the way too quickly.
The summer holiday was over.

After six weeks, the school started again. In each city, the banners hung with warnings to motorists here to point out. Children in traffic, not all, looked equally good to left and right before crossing the streets, and because of that, there happened many accidents in the first weeks after the summer holidays. At each pedestrian crossing, there were people to assist in crossing over. The plants looked thirsty in the classrooms after eight weeks of abandoning.

Every kid searched for the best table in the classroom and looked around for any new kids this year.

The new kids were doubtfully wobbling from one on the other leg back and forth. Their fear of sweat was just as pervasive as a dressing room full of rugby players after a strenuous game. For some reason, they always chose the table next to me to take place. I think they could read in a blink of an eye that I was just like them, the "misfit" of the class. They had to sit next to me on the teacher's instructions often because the popular kids already occupied all the other tables in the classroom.

No one interfered with me unless it had to or the teacher had told it. During the sport class, I was always the last one chosen. No, I wasn't exactly popular in elementary school. Everyone thought of me as a weird kid. I could not blame them. Because of the oversized clothes and small specs with a flower design on my nose, I fell entirely outside the boat. All the other girls in my class had beautiful hair, wore fashionable clothes.

The clothes that I wore went back to a century ago. And my haircut was perhaps the worst of everything. My hair was thin and greasy, and it hung lifeless along my face. If I tied it up in a tail, hairs would jump up as if I was a

walking receiving satellite. Yes, I was a particular case. Ugly? I think I was. Dumb?
I doubted that sometimes. I always thought that I was smart, but as soon as someone called me dumb, I instantly started to challenge myself. I tried not to attract too much attention.
I prefer to pull myself back in a dark corner with a thick book and left reality far behind me.
I recessed in a fantasy world. But how well I also did my best to camouflage, I was a star in failing. I tried to make a good impression, but then I let something fall out of my hands. I bumped into someone or said something stupid or just froze. When I think back to the first schooldays of my life, the fears and sweat break out again, and I feel like that little girl from then.
I still don't dare to speak in front of a large group, I try to avoid cameras, and if this doesn't work, I freeze and make myself look like a complete idiot.

The new school year started all wrong for me, really wrong. In the second school week, I got stuck between the ground and an iron plateau near a tree. While trying to get loose, I twisted my knee and could no longer stand on it. The concierge brought me to the emergency room of the nearest hospital. They directly took an X-ray of my knee and ankle, which showed that I had a small fracture in my ankle and dislocated my knee cap. My whole leg had to get wrapped in plaster. With two crutches to support, I got dropped off at home.

My foster parents helped me out of the car and thanked the man-friendly for bringing home their "daughter." They were overly sweet to me while I was in this plaster. I didn't have to do anything by myself. Suddenly, I was allowed to have dinner at the kitchen table and didn't have to do any household tasks; Cindy temporarily took these over. Cindy was not happy about this, and she let me know that very clearly.

For six weeks, she ignored me, didn't say a single word to me. I knew very well why. Jealousy! Once the plaster came off, Cindy also got her voice back. The "normal" life also started for me again.

Three weeks later, I ran to school during the lunch break on the school playground when the bell rang, and I stumbled upon someone's bag while I hurried into the row.

I felt something break when I felt on the ground and knew right away that something was wrong. While the tears on my cheeks were glowing for a moment as my pounding pulse, I shouted for help.

The Miss brought me to the Director, who called my foster parents and told them I had to go to the hospital.

Instead of taking me, they drove home, and they told me to wait in my room.

There I was, sitting in my room, waiting and hoping that they would take me to a doctor. I wanted to go to the doctor, and I wanted him to stop the pain. But Yolanda didn't think it was necessary. Yolanda thought it probably was only sprained.

'Stop whining about this. I determine whether you go to the doctor or not.'

I begged her to call, and when she finally reached the outpatient unit, asking if it could wait until tomorrow, she looked even angrier than before.

The doctor showed her that my wrist got broken in two places.

'Hm, look at that,' Yolanda said sarcastically.

The doctor walked out of the room to arrange some things he could put me back in plaster, and Yolanda turned to me.

'Don't look at me like that. You might just pull a muscle or something.'

We said goodbye to the doctor, and he said, 'it's a good thing you have come. If she had walked around like this for longer, then I couldn't help her. Next time anything like this happens, you should immediately come to us.'

Unlike last time, they didn't have the slightest compassion for me, and they gave me the assignment to clean the toilet every day. Because the plaster should not become wet, they tied a plastic bag to it. Cindy was relieved that she wasn't the only one who had to do all the house tasks.

A wrong desire

The month of November had arrived, the month in which Saint Nicholas visited our country until after his birthday on five December. Everyone was delighted, and of course, we were wondering if the Saint would come to us. We were instructed to cut toys from folders and then paste them on a blank sheet of paper.
That was supposed to become our wish list. I went diligently to work. But I could not find anything that I could ask. The master bowed over my table and looked at how far I had come. 'You haven't cut anything from toys; why is that?'
'I don't know what I have to ask,' I replied.
'Then you must have a lot of toys. It is also tricky in that case.'
He pulled his nose up contemptuously and walked on.

I could only think of another home. Somewhere where the people were kind to us. So I decided to put that on paper. That turned out to be a big mistake for me. Once the master read this, he sent me to the director.
'How dare you write such a thing like that. You should be happy with the life you have. Show some more respect for your foster parents. They provide good care for you and your little brother. Without them, you were nowhere.' The master was furious.

I sat on the seat in front of the director. In the little room hung a stale air, and there were lists of diplomas on the wall.

I looked mesmerized at the clock. It was the same clock that my father had hung on the wall at his home—a heavy wooden watch with a man who wore the globe on his shoulders. I felt sorry for that man because I knew how he must have been feeling, carrying the world's problems on his shoulders.

The director explained everything over the phone, and after the phone call, he turned his chair towards me.

'I have just spoken to them and told your parents what happened in class. They were not happy about it, but that you can probably understand that, right?'

I nodded but said nothing else.

We decided that you cannot use the library to read for two weeks, at least in consultation. You will need to earn that back. Because we don't like ungratefulness, young lady.'

I jumped off my chair and started to scream wildly. 'What? That is not true! I'm not ungrateful! Those people are not good at all. They are bad, evil. You hear me!'

I moved the chair backward and ran out of the room.

I heard the director scream something at me, but I didn't listen to what it was; I was too far.

I ran as fast as I could to the other side of the street, to my aunt's house. With my fists, I hit the door, but no one opened it. She was not at home.
What was I supposed to do now? I looked skittish over my shoulder and saw how the Director and the Concierge came running towards me. Completely out of breath, they stopped in front of me.
'Have you gone insane!' Shouted the director at me. 'You're going back inside, and you will never try this again.'
'No, you don't believe me! You are just as stupid as my foster parents!'

The Concierge grabbed my arm, and I tried in vain to disengage from his hands. He was much stronger than me and pulled me back into school. The director ran straight to his room and picked up the phone again. Now I was screwed. He went to call my foster parents and tell them what had happened. I started to vibrate violently and knew that I had lost the fight.
The Concierge kept me firmly.
'Why did you run away? You don't help yourself with such behavior.'
He looked worried at the girl next to him.
I gave no response to his questions.
I could only imagine the punishment that was ahead of me. The door opened, and the director came out of his room.

'Your parents come to pick you up. You get suspended for at least one week. I have no idea what I have to do with you. Rethink your behavior this next week. Because we do not tolerate inappropriate behavior at school.'
I kept staring silently to the ground.
My mind wandered off to my father.
When will he come and get me? I missed him and Madu so much.

I had to wait in the hallway until my foster parents arrived. The seat I was sitting on got placed so that the director could keep a close eye on me. Every time he looked through the window of his door to check if I was still sitting in my spot. A sense of powerlessness overtook me. I lost all my hope at that time. It took about half an hour before my foster parents were there.
As soon as they arrived, they went first into the boardroom. I heard the director talking to them, but about what I could not hear. My foster-parents probably claim that I lied and that I am crazy. Those thoughts alone made me wild. But that anger came out in fear as soon as they got out of the room. 'Leave this up to us,' said Yolanda to the Director.
'We will speak a hearty word to this young lady.'
Then she turned to me, 'Pack your bag and come home.'
I got up and walked with them to the car. I threw a glance at my aunt's house, hoping that she would be home by now.

'Don't even think about it,' said Peter imminent.

'We heard that you have been at their front door. We will teach you a lesson as soon as we arrive home. So you will never think of this again.'
I felt the last bit of courage sink into my shoes.
It was my entire fault. I got myself this time in a sticky situation, me and no one else!
While we drove home, I could only think of one thing: what are they going to do with me? Whatever it would be, I promised myself not to cry. Don't show any weakness. The less they could enjoy it. Once home, Peter sent me directly to my room. I didn't get it. No punishment?
After one hour, they came silently into the room; both were quiet and didn't say a word, also not to each other. Yolanda came up behind me and pulled the sweater I was wearing that day over my head. My undershirt they left on as always.
That was to prevent visible damage. So outsiders get no suspicion.
Peter had an evil look in his eyes, emotionless.
He made his belt loose and pulled this out of his shorts.
'Turn around.'
I did not respond. I remained standing where I stood as if I was frozen, petrified.
Yolanda grabbed my shoulders, turned me around, and squeezed painfully in my shoulder.

She pushed my head down. I was about crooked bent and felt the first slap.
The belt came on my back with a clanging soaking. Seconds later, another one and another one.
I couldn't breathe. I bit so hard on my lips that I tasted blood at some point. And each time before the belt hit my back, I held my breath. Only this way, I could avoid myself from crying and screaming out of pain. The sound of a whip or belt still gives me the shivers down my body. My punishment ended, and they got out of the room. I heard him say to his wife that he had earned a beer now. Yolanda took one last look at me.
'Honey, you've deserved like three of them. This tramp will think twice next time, and if she doesn't, I will kill her.'
By crawling on the floor, I eventually reached my bed.
I pulled myself into bed. I laid down on my belly. Laying on my back was now impossible.
I turned back and forth to find the right position.

I burst into tears. How long would this go on? How long could I endure? The pain, the loss of my mother, and the humiliation? My mind suddenly took a different turn, a thought that I had ignored so far. I hoisted myself gently from bed and sat a little while on edge.
I heard how my foster parents were laughing. The TV was on and pretty loud. I got up and walked towards the bathroom door. Once in the bathroom, I silently turned

the faucet open. I caught the flowing water with my hands so the water wouldn't make a sound. The bath filled itself silently with warm water. Small air bubbles floated underwater, and I wondered how a fish would feel in the Pacific Ocean. Without taking off my clothes, I stepped into the bath and laid down in the warm water. The only thing I heard underwater was my pounding heart. Would fish in the sea also experience it like this? Or do they hear many times better than us? I opened my eyes, and the view above me rippled up and down gracefully. Will it go fast? Does it hurt?
My thoughts raced through my mind.
I can't go on like this, no more pain.
I want it to stop. Thinking of my mother and the words of Yolanda: 'now she doesn't have to feel ashamed for her retarded children.' Everyone was better off. Better off without me.
Small air bubbles tinkled at my nostrils. All of a sudden, I saw Yolanda above me. She came fast approaching and pulled me with a hard jerk out of the water.
I forgot to hold my breath.
'What were you doing, idiot.' Her voice sounded far away.
I sneezed and coughed water and gasped.
The bath mat got soaked because of me, and I heard her railing in the distance. I did not respond. The only thing I wanted was to go back into the water and away from this existence. My hair pasted stuck to my forehead.

'Take your clothes immediately off,' she screamed wildly.
A stinging pain brought me back to reality, and she had lashed out at my face. She threw a towel around me and sent me to bed. Once I hit the pillow, it got soaked by the bathwater, mixed with my tears that disappeared in the pillowcase.

I had terrible headaches and tried to get some sleep until Robbie came back from school. He went to our school for the first time. He turned five years old in January. And that is why he was allowed to run from the mid-November trial in kindergarten. As soon as he and the others came home, the daily activities started for me.
'Sissy? Sis?' I heard someone whisper in my ear.
As soon as I opened my eyes, I saw him standing next to my bed.
'Hey, you're already at home? How was school?'
A smile appeared on his face, and he put his thumb up proudly. On the other hand, he held a drawing.
'Is that for me?' I asked him curiously. Robbie nodded and held out his arm to me. I took the drawing from him and looked at it. 'You have made a beautiful drawing, and I'm proud of you!'
As proud as a Peacock, he left the room again to go back to his room.
 I felt immensely proud, and I was so pleased to be his sister.

There was no other best brother in the world than him.
I tried to sit up straight. It wasn't that easy.

'Hi!' cheered Kim cheerfully.
'Hi.'
'Oh, no. What happened to you?' Kim looked worried and observed the damage.
'What have you done wrong this time?'
Casually I pulled up my shoulders.
'Is not important.'
'Not important? Did you see how you look right now?'
Then Cindy also entered the room: 'Oops.'
'I made a mistake. At school, we had to make a wish list, and I could not invent anything in terms of toys. So I wrote on the piece of paper that I would like to have another home, where they will be gentle with me.'
'And then?' Cindy asked me.
'And then the master read it and became evil. The director has called up our foster parents, and the rest you see is the result.'
'You shouldn't tell anyone. Nobody will believe you anyway. They believe only whatever the adults tell them.'
Kim and Cindy looked at each other, and both nodded.
'I also know this now,' I said and let out a deep sigh.
I was silent about my suicide attempt. That wasn't the girl's business.

Kim and Cindy were sisters, and that was obvious.

They both had dark blonde hair. Gray-green eyes, and both had many freckles on their faces.

Cindy was one year older than Kim. Kim was the sweetest of both of them. An empathetic girl with a big heart. Cindy was more elaborate. Played nice in your face, but could be backstabbing too.

I was the type of girl that is quiet, shy, and reluctant.

I prefer to stay still and unknown. But don't try to hurt my baby brother. Then I was no longer afraid and reticent. Then I said whatever came up in my mind.

That part of me often brought me into trouble, and as soon as I noticed a trail of injustice, I became wild. I was righteous and hated it when people lied or cheated.

I could kill Cindy when she blames someone else; if she had done something wrong, she slid it right on another person. Then, of course, I went against it and eventually got the beating I intended to endure.

Yolanda entered the room and asked to accompany Cindy.

Kim looked surprised in their direction, and then she looked back at me.

'What's the matter?' she asked.

'I have no idea,' I replied.

After a few minutes, they came back. Cindy held a large piece of chocolate in her right hand. It looked delicious.

Kim looked with wide eyes at the delicacy.

Yolanda asked her: 'Do you also want a piece of this?'
She nodded yes and held out her hand.
The next moment she screamed, Yolanda had knocked her down to the ground.
'Dirty pig…'

I jumped up from my bed and hit as hard as I could with both of my fists on Yolanda's back.
'Leave her alone,' I screamed, 'stay away from her, bitch.'
I kept yelling at her until she had left the room.
'Please calm down. I'm here, and Yolanda is gone.' I took Kim, who lay huddled on the ground, into my arms, and tried to reassure her.
'She's already gone,' I whispered into her ear.
I was furious. I turned to Cindy.
'What the hell happened, and why did she hit her?'
She shrugged her shoulders but did not answer.
'I don't understand. Kim is your little sister. Why are you doing this? Why don't you say or do anything about it?'
That made me so angry. I couldn't understand this. Why?
'I don't dare; I am scared,' she replied, embarrassed.
I kept my thoughts to myself, but at that time, I just wanted to shout at her that she was a coward.
Despite that, I very well understood her fear. I was disgusted by her. 'Go away.'
I helped Kim stand up and saw how Yolanda had left her handprint on that little cheek. Her glasses sat askew on her nose. I pushed him gently with a finger straight onto

her nose. I felt sorry for her. Kim was a sweet girl that didn't do anything wrong. She would never hurt anyone, and yet that bitch hit her.

I had to do something. I had to make sure that we got out from here, away from these people, these beasts.

The escape

I peered at the white granular ceiling tiles above my bed. My mind could only think about the outbreak, running away, and finding a safer home. But how did I approach this? Busy pondering, I fell asleep. The next morning started, and Yolanda came stomping our room. Her eyes spat fire, and she had small white flakes layers spit on her lips. Without saying a word, she dragged us all out of bed and pulled the blinds open. Then I noticed something.
There were no locks on the windows. I could open them. That allowed us to escape from this hell.
It was a good plan. My heart made a jump of excitement. I tried to hide it and tried not to show any of it to Yolanda. We had to dress up and get ready for school.
During the lessons, I had to try my best to keep my focus. I caught myself several times, drifting off.
I came up with all kinds of plans on how it had to be done and thought about the right time. The whole week I was working on it. I was aware that we had only one chance to get away.
The weekend arrived, and I concluded that Saturday morning would be the right time. Then our foster parents always slept very long, and if we did, they would not even notice that we ran off.

No one knew of my plans at home; I had deliberately kept quiet about it.
The plan should not end up at my foster parents.

Jimmy and Cindy were nowhere Saturday morning, and I had searched for them everywhere. Kim was still asleep, so she didn't know where they went.
Suddenly we heard a gently knocking on our window. It scared the hell out of me.
The blinds were set aside by a hand, and we saw one leg come in through the window. Then we saw who it was. Cindy stuck her head through the blinds and laughed about meeting us. I was not the only one with a plan.
'Look what I've brought for us.'
In her right hand, she held a big bag of bread rolls.
'We stole this from the store,' boasted Jimmy tougher.
'They didn't catch us.'
'Yes,' Cindy nodded.
'Jimmy came up with the idea. We were so hungry, and it still takes so much time before mom and dad awake.'
I could not believe my ears. Jimmy and Cindy had stolen bread rolls.
'You both are insane. What if you get caught? What then, huh?'
'But that didn't happen,' answered Jimmy.
'No, but it could've happened. Don't do this again,' I tried to warn Jimmy and Cindy.
Cindy looked up to me now.

'Aren't you hungry then?'
'Yes, of course, I am, but they beat you to death if they figure this out.'
Jimmy pushed a roll in my hand.
'Keep your mouth shut and eat.'
We feasted on delicious sandwiches, and in minutes we ate all of them. While I went to pee, Jimmy and Cindy decided to go back for more. They climbed through the window.

When I entered the bedroom, I saw Kim nervous at the window.
'Where are they?'
Kim turned and pointed outside.
'Oh no, you can't be serious?!' I was furious. That stupid idea could ruin my plan.
They took so long to return home.
I decided to tell Kim about my plan. While I told her everything, her eyes were getting bigger, and her face turned white.
'I don't know if I dare to run away, Elisa,' she stammered.
'Of course, you do; you don't want to stay here, right? They treat us like animals. We must get out of here, or they will beat us to death someday.'
Kim was still not entirely convinced, but she didn't want to stay behind.
I started with the first steps of my plan.

I pulled out my baby brother and Mees from their room and took them to ours. They had to be in my area. Because as soon as Jimmy and Cindy were back, we would run away from this hell.

I packed everyone's favorite stuffed animal in my backpack. Everyone got dressed up, and we were ready to go.

Kim kept guard at the door, and she listened if she heard someone awake. I looked worried outside to see if they came back. But they didn't come back.

I started to worry even more. The ominous feeling in my belly came back, just like always, if there was something wrong.

Suddenly the doorbell rang, and we heard how our foster father opened the door.

We tried to find out who it was at the door with our ears against the bedroom door. After a few minutes, the front door shut with a slam.

The bedroom door flew open, and Yolanda stormed into our room. We had to follow her directions to the living room.

Once we walked in, we saw Jimmy and Cindy.

'Who knew about this?' roared Peter.

Silent ruled the room.

'Who?' He shouted again.

He looked at us with a feral look. No one made a sound.

I looked to the right of me where Kim was standing. The poor child was shaking in her legs. Her glasses hung askew on the tip of her nose. I realized all too well that someone had to blame, and otherwise, we would stand there all day long.

When I wanted to put my finger into the air and take the blame, Cindy stepped forward. Startled and amazed, I looked at her and shook my head as unobtrusively as possible.

But she didn't see it.

'Jimmy and I did it. The rest didn't know anything about this. I swear.'

Peter turned to her and waved his arm up. Cindy popped down just in time, whereby he missed her.

He wobbled and got out of balance.

He landed with his hip on the sharp corner of the table. That had to hurt a lot.

'Go to your room!' He shouted.

Breakfast was something that belonged to the past since that day. On the weekend we got the only dinner. That was our punishment for what they had done.

Most people do not know how real hunger feels. Being hungry is something completely different than wanting to eat a snack. People who live below the poverty line are hungry. The homeless outside is suffering from hunger.

The children, who search for leftovers in waste bins in third world countries, will starve from hunger.

We learned the true meaning of the word.

That same afternoon there were locks on the windows. Our foster parents wanted to be sure we didn't do anything like that ever again. As a result, my plan broke into pieces. Now we could no longer escape through the windows. I was so freaking mad at Jimmy and Cindy.

They had no idea what kind of problems they had caused with their stunt. There was nothing else to do then to rethink a new plan.

The nights afterward, I lay awake, and then I fantasized about how we were going to escape from this hell. With the sweat on our foreheads and a tower high heart rate, we ran through the streets of our neighborhood, looking for a safe place to hide. I always saw the globe-shaped houses that stand in our community. We tucked us in the bushes to see if nobody followed us. We were away, escaped, and safe, but what's next? Where did we have to go?

Where did we have to live? And what if the weather got colder outside, we couldn't sleep in snow and cold. I felt lost, and this could never work.

Maybe we had to run away, but living on the street was not an option.

I could not take care of all the children, and no one else would help us because the people would bring us immediately back to the foster home. With these disturbing thoughts, I eventually fell asleep. It took a long time before I had gathered the courage to get back to running away. The days go by like normal, until that particular day. We all got neat clothing, and Yolanda asked us to put them on.

'Come with me, please, follow me.'

Yolanda led us to the living room. There I saw the lady who had brought us here. 'I have a surprise for you all,' Nell said. 'Today, we're going to have some fun, and you will come with me.'

We looked at each other, all shocked.

'What are we going to do?' Kim asks with a soft voice.

'That you will see, otherwise it is not a surprise anymore, right?'

We all obediently nodded our heads.

The car journey took a long time, but we were all delighted. We sang songs from the full chest and speculated with all our imagination where we were going.

'Maybe we'll go to the Zoo, and I find animals so sweet.' Kim clapped delightedly in her hands.

'I think we're going to the movies,' said Jimmy. Robbie was staring outside the car window with a massive smile on his face, and he enjoyed the drive.

'Are you having fun?' I asked him.

He turned and looked at me, 'Yeah.'

Once we had arrived at our destination, we saw a large building.

'What are we going to do here?' Jimmy got impatient with every second.

Nell laughed, 'you had guessed this right.'

Jimmy cheered, 'you see, I knew it. We are going to the cinema.'

Now the rest of the kids also started to cheer.

Mega large posters hung inside the building with lions on them.

"Now, in the cinema, the Lion King!"

A sweet little cub stood with his father proudly on a rock. I didn't know why, but I felt an intense report on this image. I longed for my parents, to the campground.

I just wanted to be with them.

'Elisa, why are you crying?' Nell bent towards me.

'Nothing!' I snapped and turned evil to her. What a stupid question, she did this to us! She had brought us to these people, and now she thinks she can make it right by taking us to the movie. I don't think so. I watched the film with a bad feeling in my stomach. This feeling got intense at the moment that Simba's father got trampled by a herd of stampeding buffaloes and died. Tears ran down my cheeks. I felt sorry for Simba, who was left alone without any family. Except Scar, his evil uncle who had decided that he was the culprit, pointed at him guilty for the death of his father.

I just had to think about what Yolanda said to us after telling us about our mother's death. It was my entire fault.

'Stop acting like that.' Nell looked irritated at me, 'I'm doing this for you, the next time you can stay home. If you can't behave, then you don't deserve to do something fun as well.'
'I don't care! Do you think you can make everything right by taking us to the movie? I don't think so!' I was so mad at her.
'What do you mean? I wanted to surprise you all with a fun excursion.'
'Yeah, sure,' I muttered.
Finally, the movie paused for a moment. Now we could all go to the bathroom, and we got a cold drink and a packet of crisps.

I had to sit next to Nell for the rest of the movie. I kept an eye on her. She seemed very disappointed, and I started to feel guilty.
'I'm sorry, it's not your fault.'
'What do you mean anyway? What is not my fault?' she asked.
I hesitated; should I tell her what they did to us? No.
'Never mind.'
She would not believe us like the others and tell our foster parents about the crap she had heard, and I could count on a beating again.
'Why are you acting this strange?' Nell looked at me and shook her head.

After the movie, we drove back home; everyone fell asleep, and I could see the sunset's red-orange glow. The sun sank slowly in the distance and disappeared into the ground.
'Thank you so much for today.'
I looked at Nell, who concentrated on the traffic on the road.
'My little brother liked it very much. I could tell from the smile on his face. It didn't come off for one second.'
'You love your little brother very much, right. That is beautiful; a family is the most important thing in life.'

I understood what she meant, he meant the world to me, and I would not know what to do without him.
'Why have you brought us to these people?'
'Your mother had asked us for help. She could no longer provide for your concerns. There was no money for food or new clothes for you. And for this reason, I came to pick you both up, and I brought you to them.'
'I remember that,' I whispered.
It was deadly quiet in the car. Everyone was still in a deep sleep. Now and then, you could hear someone snoring. Jimmy was bothered by a cold that he had suffered the previous week at running away barefoot. We made a turn and drove to our street, and I woke up, Robbie gently.
'Wake up, brother, we are at home.'
He looked at me. 'I don't want to go home.'

'Me too, but we are already there. But I promise you, and we will get out of here soon,' I whispered into Robbie's ear so that Nell couldn't hear me.

'And how did it go? Did they behave themselves?' Peter turned to Nell and asked if he could offer her a cup of tea.

'No, thank you. It's late, and I have to go. But all the kids were delightful, all of them. In my opinion, they enjoyed the surprise very much.'

Everyone voted full. I looked and waited for the moment Nell would tell them how revolted I had behaved myself. She winked, and with a smile, she bows to me.

'Our secret,' she whispered and wrapped her arms around me.

I was grateful to her. She didn't know that she saved me from punishment. I can go to sleep comfortably in the knowledge that they are not going to beat me. Once Nell had closed the door behind her, we had to go to bed. This time it didn't take long until I fell asleep. That night I slept like a baby.

The following day Yolanda came in and asked us all to gather in the living room. First, I had to give Robbie a clean diaper; even though he was five years old, he still wore a diaper because they didn't potty trained him,

'Sis?' He looked anxiously at the door before he continued.

'Have you been naughty?'

I shrugged on. 'For, as far as I know, I didn't. Maybe Yolanda and Peter have something important to tell. Don't worry; nothing is going to happen to you.'

We got placed in a row of the dining table, and there was a knock on the door. Yolanda opened the door, and a man came in.
'Here they are, take your pick.'
How did she refer to: take your pick.
I took a step forward and pushed my little brother, so he completely disappeared behind my back.
'Don't you think they are too young? How old are these kids?'
The man seemed to feel uncomfortable and made a nervous impression. A pungent sweat smell came to meet us at the moment that he leans towards us. It stank so much that I almost started to gag.
'Act normal for once, tramp!'
She grabbed my arm and flung me to the ground.
'I think she is sick,' said the unknown man. 'I'm going home; I changed my mind. That was a bad idea.'
The man turned around, and Yolanda rushed after him.
'Don't worry and please stay, she's not sick, and she is also the oldest. She is already thirteen years old.'
'She is lying, and I'm not thirteen years old! I am ten!' I shouted and was determined to thwart her plan.
'Why did you come here? And what did she mean with, 'take your pick?'

The shame became visible on his jaws, and he ran out of the door.
'You are such a dirty tramp.' Yolanda was furious and beat me several times with her flat hand on my face.
'Now you have screwed this up! You finally got the chance to make yourself useful. He was going to pay me a lot of money! You are going to pay for it!'
The other kids ran to their rooms and were hiding under the covers. They could hear the hysterical screams coming from the living room, and they could count how often they beat me; they struck me that day. I crawled back to my room.
My whole back had bruises.
I went through hell in pain.
'Why do you have a big mouth? You know you get beaten up by them when you do that.' Cindy helped me get in bed.
'That man was about to do something horrible to us, I felt that. And if I had said nothing, something bad would happen to one of us.'
'You don't know that he seemed nice to me. Maybe mom is right about you, and you ruin everything.' Cindy was mad at me and said it was my fault that Yolanda had beat me like this.

She didn't speak one single word to me for at least one week. She ignored me and sucked up to our foster parents by playing nice to them. But I was sure I had made the right choice and the punishment...?

I could barely move for one week. The terrible muscle pain and the tender spots on my back reminded me long about the occurrence. My foster mother called me sick at school the next day. I had severe pneumonia; I was ahead on some of the learning material after all. Only when the bruising was gone entirely I was allowed to go back to school.

During those weeks, they made sure that I didn't have to feel bored. They wrote a long list of household chores so that they could sit down on the couch with their lazy asses. Cleaning, ironing, vacuuming, and wiping all rooms, bathroom, and cleaning kitchen cabinets.

When I finished my chores, I had to start all over again.

I learned how to run a household at a very young age. It became the most normal thing in the world, and I didn't mind doing it.

I dreamed a thousand miles away while I brushed the floors. Sometimes I was so far away that I didn't even notice when the others came home from school.

I traveled around the world, ate, and drank the best dishes and drinks. Swim in a large blue ocean along with my little brother and lay down in the sun on the most beautiful white beaches that you can imagine. My dreams kept me going during that difficult time. It was my only way out of the hell I found myself in.

The first day I went to school, it turned into a fiasco. My only and best friend was thrilled that I was back again and hugged me. I smiled bravely, but inwardly I was dying of desire to tell her my secret. I couldn't keep my tears away.

'What's wrong? Why are you crying?' Tessa was my best friend at the time. Very skinny girl. With a pointed nose and her oversized glasses.

She also often gets teased. During the break, we stayed close together so that the kids left us alone.

'Flu and pneumonia,' I muttered.

'Oh, that's not good. But I'm glad you are feeling better again. Without you, I have no fun.'

I had to laugh; her words caused a warm feeling in my body.

It felt amicable and familiar. It was the same feeling as when I saw my father again. During the break, I decided to tell her about how my foster parents treated us. We looked for a quiet place at the climbing frame, and I told her about what had happened.

Tessa was stunned, and as soon as the bell rang, she stood up.

'I write to you in return.' She turned and ran into the school—the rest of the day, she ignored me. During the math courses, there was a note going around through the class that was for me. I could see that the handwriting came from Tessa.

The text read as follows:

'I'm sure you made this up just to make sure I feel sorry for you. But I don't believe those lies. Your mom already warned me about your lies. Your mom does no such thing. You are a filthy liar, and I don't want anything to do with you.'

I turned to her and shouted through the classroom: 'she is not my mother!'

I started to lose all courage and was wondering whether I could escape from here. The prospect was dark and disconsolate. It lasted a total of almost six years, filled with neglect, mental and physical abuse. In these years, I experienced the worst pains and intense pleasures as soon as I saw my father.

The abuse fumbled my value—self-hatred, disgust, insecure. I was useless, unimportant to everyone: an ugly, stupid, and dumb child. I often asked God the question, why I was born. Why did God not help me?

So many questions, and I never got an answer. I lived only for one reason: one reason that prevented me from trying a suicidal attempt once more to escape this hell. The strength to go on, I found that strength in love for my little brother.

The 25th of December 1995, the day the whole world celebrated Christmas. The day every kid has been waiting on. While we stayed in our rooms, we speculated about what Santa Claus would give us as presents.

Saint Nicholas had forgotten about us on the 5th of December, so we hoped for Santa Claus to bring us a gift.

'Oh, I hope I get a new doll this year!' Kim yelled excitedly.

Cindy dreamed about new Barbie's and craft supplies.

I was hoping fervently on a set of crayons so that I could make new drawings. The first would be for my father and Madu.

It lasted an eternity, but in the end, we gathered in the living room. We were in shock. Santa sat down on a chair in our living room, and he beckoned us closer.

'Come to me, little children.'

Delighted, but also anxiously, we slowly shuffled closer.

'Who wants to sit on my lap?' the best man asked us.

Everyone looked at each other.

Jimmy showed courage and went for us.

'So, young man. Tell Santa if you behave like a good kid this year?' Jimmy looked at our foster parents, who were sitting on the couch.

'Yes, of course,' they answered Santa.

So we all sat down on his lap, and once Santa Claus left to another family, it was time to open the presents. With a smile, Yolanda grabbed deep in the big bag, which Santa had left for us. We all got a pencil and a chocolate bar.

We looked at each other.

'Don't we get more?' Jimmy was disappointed.

'Do you not get enough?' she snapped vehemently. 'Go to your rooms, ungrateful bastards!'
And so we turned back to our rooms.
We were not ungrateful children, but the disappointment was there when we realized our wishes did not come true.

'Get me out of here!'

10 January 1996
I lived for six years with these horrible people. The years had crawled by, and with every day passed by, a piece of my soul disappeared. My image distorted my self-image, self-esteem was nowhere to find, and I turned from a happy girl into an empty shell. Longing for death, lonely and broken by all the suffering that got inflicted upon me. Until one day,
Nell Vermaars surprised us with a visit, and I could hear that the tempers got high between her and my foster parents. After a while, Yolanda came in and told me to put on my best clothes.

With best clothes, she means a black and white striped jumper with Minnie Mouse and black legging. When I had changed my clothes, I ran to the living room. Nell was sitting there waiting for me, and she had a surprise for me. The faces of my foster parents spoke volumes.

They were not happy with the unexpected visit from Nell. Before I walked to the door, Peter called me to him.

'Don't you dare to open your mouth and tell her anything, or I kill your brother,' he whispered with a vicious look in his eyes.

I was terrified and nodded obediently. Nell was already behind the wheel and had the engine started. I crawled on the passenger seat and searched for the belt. My hands trembled with fear that I failed in this a couple of times.

'Come on. I'm doing it just for you.' She picked up the belt and made it tight.

'Thank you,' I said gently.

'Have you been wondering where we're going?' she asked me.

I nodded, 'are we going to the cinema again?'

'No, not this time. It is a much bigger surprise.'

'To the beach?' She had aroused my curiosity.

'You'll see when we're there,' she replied, smiling.

Internally I had great concern about Robbie; what if they hurt him while I was gone.

Suddenly I said: 'I don't want to go with you. I want to go back, and I want to go home right now.'

My thoughts went to my little brother. Rampage and fear took the upper hand. I started to cry and begged Nell to

turn the car around and drive home. Nell was confused about my behavior.
'Why don't you want to spend a few hours with me? I'll bring you back home again.'
I could not tell her why I wanted so badly to go home, they would do something to my little brother, and I had to prevent that. I wiped the tears with my sleeve from my face and decided to calm myself.
I repeatedly told myself that nothing would happen to Robbie while I was gone. That helped to calm me down.
The car stopped for a large building. I had never been there before and was wondering where I was.

'So sweet girl, are you ready?'
I turned to her and looked at Nell; she was a kind woman of middle age. When she laughed, little wrinkles appeared around her eyes and mouth corners. She had a sweet smile, a smile that reassured people.
I think I started to like her a little bit more.
I took a deep breath and opened the door. We walked together, holding hands towards the building. Inside we got greeted by people who seemed to work there.
'Here we go up the stairs.'
A beautiful cherry wooden staircase with red carpet, which ran up three floors high. High walls and ceilings with crystal chandeliers. I had not seen anything so beautiful. Breathtaking.

I was amazed and greeted everyone I met. While I ran up the stairs, I felt like a true Queen, and in my mind, I lived here along with Robbie and with lackeys who served whatever we asked them to work. On the second floor, Nell stopped for two large wooden doors.

'In here you find your surprise, you have an hour. Have a lot of fun.'
As soon as I walked into the room, I could not believe my eyes.
'Mommy!'
'Sweetie! Oh, my dear, I missed you so much!'
I ran to her, she threw her arms around me and lifted me.
That could not be true; my mother was dead. Was this all a dream? I squeezed my eyes tightly, but as soon as I opened them, I was still in my mother's arms, and I started to cry.
'Why are you crying, sweetie?'
'They told me that you were dead. You didn't want to live because of us.'
I gasped, my throat hurt, and it was hard to swallow.
'What? What do you tell me now? Who said that? Are they completely insane?'
She put me down and sat on a chair.
'Who said so?' she asked, shocked.
'Yolanda and Peter,' I replied and crawled at her on her lap.

She kept silent and looked shocked at me. Her face turned pale.

I felt a primal force inside and decided to tell her my biggest secret. She grabbed her face with both of her hands and burst into tears.
'Oh, Sweetie, I am so sorry. I never knew this before. I promise you I will do everything to get you away from there. You and Robbie.' She put her arms around me and pulled me closer.
I heard how her heart railed. We continued to sit like that for a while, without talking to each other. The door opened, and Nell entered the room.
'Do you have any idea how my children get treated there?' Mama jumped up from her seat and stormed to Nell.
Nell was frightened and tried to calm her down in the first place.
My mother spits fire like a mad bull.
'Quiet, quiet, please. Calm down because I don't understand anything of what you are trying to say.' Nell grabbed a Chair and beckoned me to come so that I could explain.
'They hit us every day, and I need to clean all day. We rarely play outside and get very little to eat.'
I initially realized that she didn't believe me; I also told her about what Peter said to me just before our departure.

Her facial expression changed.
'Was this the reason why you didn't want to come with me?'
There was a vibration audible in her voice.
I nodded, 'I don't want them to harm my baby brother, and when I'm with him, I can protect him. I am afraid that something bad will happen to him. Please help us, Mrs. Vermaars. Help us!'
Nell stood up and asked my mother to follow her. A few minutes later, a young woman came into the room and asked me if I wanted to play a game.
'Where is my mommy?'
'She is with Mrs. Nell talking about you. I promise you, and she will come back soon.' I was worried, and she could read it from my face.
'We can play a game in the meanwhile, what do you think of that?'
I didn't want to play a game, but I obeyed and chose a match from the shelf in the room's corner. When I put the box on the table, my eyes noticed a square object. It was a big box with gift wrap paper around it. There was also a note on, for my honeybee—a pet name for me, created by my mother. Curious, I ran to it and looked at it carefully.
What would be in it, I asked myself.
'Do you think I can open it?' I asked the young woman.
'If your name is on it, it is fixed.'

I started gently to the corners of the tape. Pieces of bright pink gift-paper fell to the ground while I unpacked.
'Wow, a Barbie camper!'
I had seen it on television, during the advertising, but I never thought I would get one. Delighted, I pulled the box open, took out the camper, and put it on the table—a bright pink trailer with all the trimmings.
'Can we play with this, please?'
With my dearest look, I looked up to her.
'Of course, the camper is much more fun than a boring game.' the lady answered.
We decorated the camper and placed all the little shot glasses and plates in the small kitchenette cabinets.
Mom and Nell came back, and Nell said: 'say goodbye to your mother. I have to bring you back.'
'No, I don't want to go back. I want you to pick up Robbie, and I want to go home with mama!'

'That is impossible, the honeybee. Mama has to go now, but I'll see you soon.'
My mom holds me to her. I pressed myself as firmly as possible against her.
'When they find out that I have betrayed them, they hit me to death and Robbie too!' I screamed and panicked.
'Please, don't leave me again,' I begged again. The lady picked up my arms and separated me from my mother.
And then she left.

Nell stopped the car in front of the entrance of our apartment.

'Our secret,' she assured me one more time.

I was so damn nervous and anxious at that time and scared to death that they found out I told Nell, and the longer we stayed there, the more that opportunity was present.

'Promise you to come soon to get us?'

Nel promised.

I took a deep breath and walked towards the door. Peter opened the door even before we had ring the doorbell.

'I saw you guys coming.'

Of course, I thought. Peter had been waiting for us the whole time.

'Did she behave herself?' Yolanda asked with a sweet voice. They were both as easy as a lamb.

'Yes, very much,' answered Nell. 'Elisa behaved herself like an angel.'

Yolanda and Peter looked at each other. 'That's great to hear. We know how annoying she can be. Also, at school, lying and cheating are terrible.'

I looked at Nell.

She nodded compassionately with her head.

'I know what kind of hard task you have as foster parents. Those children are often doing wrong. Brutal Villeneuve.'

They were visibly relieved, reassured by her words.

'Well, absolutely, it is not easy, you know. The remaining ungrateful dogs, whatever we do for them, is never enough. Give them the finger, and then they take your whole hand.'

I could no longer listen to those hypocrites and asked them if I could go to my room. While I closed the living room door behind me, I heard them complain about those pesky foster children and what misery we brought to them. In the room, Cindy and Kim were busy playing with a Barbie and a doll.

'Are you back again?' they asked in unison.

'Yes.' I wanted to tell them what had happened that afternoon, but I had to keep my mouth shut. So no one could screw this up, and Nell could do her work undisturbed.

Robbie was sleeping, and I decided not to wake him.

I gave him gently a little kiss on his pale cheek. 'Sleep well, the little brother of mine. I love you.'

Nell didn't break her promise because, within two days, she came back.

Redemption

Date 12 January 1996, it was my brother's birthday.
They didn't make much effort to celebrate our birthdays, except for the picture moment. But that day, they hung garlands, and we could all watch TV.
The door opened, and Nell stepped in. She beckoned me to come. I obeyed her, stood up, and ran to her.
'Sweet girl, today I'm going to bring you somewhere else.'
My heart made a jump of relief.
I called my little brother with me.
'No, Elisa, not Robbie, only you.'
What? Did she get to be kidding me? I can't leave him behind. What if they hurt him while I'm gone.
'No, I'm not going without him!' I screamed and panicked. I felt the first tears roll.
'No, I'm not going with you! Forget it! Please, let us stay together. I promise you, and I'll do whatever you want. But let me stay with him.'
Nell felt sorry for me but could not accept it. She assured me that he would go to a lovely woman and be the next child to leave that horrible place. It took a while before I calmed down and eventually agreed to leave him behind. With pain in my heart, I ran up to him. There he sat, a little boy with blond hair, blue eyes, and the sweetest smile of the world. God, I loved him so much.

'Robbie, please come to me.' He listened and did what I asked. I pulled him on my lap and began to cry.

'I am so sorry. I have to go. But tomorrow, you will be picked up, and Nell will bring you to somebody that is very sweet for you.'

I started to cry even more. 'I wish I could stay with you.'

Robbie listened to me and grabbed my face with both of his hands.

'I love you so much, never forget that.' I told him one more time.

He seemed to understand me as he gently whispered goodbye and gave a little kiss on my cheek. I didn't want to leave him behind. He would get picked up the next day, and they could still do something wrong to him.

I turned myself to the vilest people I knew and looked them straight in their eyes. Full of hate and anger, I spoke out loud a promise.

'If you dare to hurt my little brother while he is still here, one day, I will kill you. Once I grow up, I'll come after you, hunt you down, and let you experience the worst pain ever written.'

Even before they could respond, Nell intervened.

'I think Elisa has spoken enough.'

After I said goodbye to all my foster brothers and sisters, I took Robbie once again in my arms.

'Whatever happens, I love you. I will come to you soon. Please never forget that you are the most important thing in the world for me. I love you.'

At the time I closed the door behind me, my heart broke into a thousand pieces. Still, even though I felt defeated, broken, and trampled. I got rescued by Nell, which gave me the strength to continue.

I had no idea where she brought me, but I promised myself: No one would ever get the chance to hurt me again.

We pitched along Avenue with tall trees and approached a large white mansion. I wondered where Nell brought me to.

'Are you nervous?' Nell looked aside and put her hand on my shoulder. I nodded.

'You will be alright, don't worry.'

'That's what you said six years ago, and look where I ended up.'

Epilogue

She brought me to a boarding school on the edge of a forest. On a plate, it said: Maria Rabboni.
This boarding school had seven family houses. They had all their names. The family home where I had to go was called Fiesole.
It took a while before I got used to my new home.
Since I had felt locked up for years, I had to learn a lot, even playing outside because, besides the campsite, I didn't feel safe outside my room.
I was anxious and withdrawn. The leaders
I put a lot of effort into gaining my confidence, even though I didn't always make it easy for them.
After a while, I found my way.
Gradually I flourished from a timid wallflower to a luxurious rose.

Unfortunately, not all misery stopped.
For years I remained bullied by schoolmates. The reason? I still don't know. They swung every day, insulting and humiliating words to my head. I was stupid, ugly, dirty, fat, etc.
They were waiting for me after schooltime to pick on me and beat me up, which happened several times a week.
No, my schooltime is not a pleasant time to look back on.

Fortunately, I loved reading, and I studied psychology. It fascinated me so much that the human brain works and where particular behavior comes from traumatic experiences.
People sometimes ask if the past is still haunting me.
The answer is: Fortunately, not anymore.
I don't hate my foster parents anymore because of what they have done to us.
I would shake hands with them if I encountered them.
I believe that my past shaped me into the woman I am today—a woman whose heart is in the right place and strong enough to survive independently.
Why do I think this?
Years later, life would put me to the test again, even harder than I had to go through before.

At the age of five, my eldest son got diagnosed with a sporadic and life-threatening blood disease.
Familial Hemophagocytic lymphohistiocytosis.
A disease that is similar to leukemia, and he had to get chemotherapy and stem cell transplantation.
This period was extremely tough.
There is nothing worse than to witness your child suffering, and you can't take it over from him nor make it go away.
Right after my son's diagnosis, my marriage to my children's father came to an end, and my dear Madu died because of Alzheimer's Disease.

So much happened that time, as a single mother of three, with one child fighting for his life and no family support, I was back in survival mode.

My son wasn't very fortunate. After the stem cell transplant, he got diagnosed with BOOP, a rare grave versus host reaction because of the stem cells.
His cells kept attacking his healthy lung tissue, even though there was no virus to attack. Because of this, he ended up in a wheelchair, with permanent oxygen to help him breathe.
There was nothing the doctors could do for him, and I got told to say goodbye to my son. He could not win this fight.
Forget everything; nothing is worse than hearing this, and looking at your precious child, feeling helpless.
I prayed to God countless times; I begged him for a miracle.
My son was still conscious, while the doctors couldn't explain this. My son should be, according to the doctors, in a comatic sleep. But somehow, he wasn't.
He was a real miracle, and I believe that his determination to survive kept him alive and awake.
On a Monday morning in the hospital, I woke up and found my son looking at me. With his little hand, he stroked down my cheek and whispered: 'Mom, I decided

to stay alive... I can't miss you nor my brother and sister.'

I answered him: 'If anyone can do it, you are that one. So let's do this!'

He remained stable while waiting for a donor's lungs.

On 4 August 2012, we got the most precious gift in the world: new lungs for my dear son. That gave him a chance at extended life.

After going through all this, my body and mind couldn't handle more.

On some day in 2014, at the age of 29, I could barely speak, walk, or see. It became clear after almost two years of intensive research of doctors and what had happened, I had a small lacunar brain attack.

I got forced to take a step back and take care of myself. I wasn't that good at it. I could care for the whole world, but when it came up to me. I couldn't.

I had to quit my job and was bound to the four walls of my home.

My body forced me to take a look inside myself, literally because of the attack, my left eyes turned inside, and I suffered from severe double vision, which made things not easy for me. Picking up a glass of water turned out to be a daily challenge.

Oh well, seeing double also has a positive side. I was enjoying the starry sky twice as much as anyone else.

I still remember a summer evening where we all sat outside in the garden.
We looked at the sky that was full of stars, at least for me. I was amazed by
how impressive the starry sky that evening used to be.
All eyes were on me, and my son wondered if I was feeling sick. There were just a few stars, according to him, there was nothing special about it.
I thoroughly enjoyed that evening on my own!
Unfortunately, we do not choose our lives. Life happens to us, and we must try to make the best of it. Setbacks and smashing
Highlights: We can learn something from both, and often they make us stronger.

Fortunately, Robbie ended up okay. After he was picked up by Nel the next day,
He went to live with Ineke, his "vacation mother." She took care of him as if he were her son.
She was his saving angel, and I am forever grateful for her excellent care.
Unfortunately, she is no longer among us; she died a few years ago from the effects of cancer.
It's nice to see that a lot of her lives on in Robbie. Thanks to her, many children in need got the love and care they needed.
We will never forget her and remain forever grateful.
Two years after writing: "Get me out of here!"

So much has changed in my life that I decided to mention this in the new book.
Let me start at the beginning!
After I published the Dutch version of this book, it already became quickly picked up by the Dutch media, and I got invited to attend one of the biggest talk-show in the Netherlands, PAUW.
I gave several interviews in newspapers and magazines, which faced me with internal fear and insecurity, and it became clear to me that I had to do something about this.
I asked myself why I had such difficulty to express myself about what had happened to me. I found out that this had to do with uncertainty, kind of doubt if the story was entirely based on the truth.
I was, after all, a child at the time, and children sometimes interpret things differently. I also had nobody to verify my story. I had no idea where the other kids went after I left the foster home.
That changed after a broadcast from "Hart van Nederland" a Dutch news broadcast, in which I had a short interview to the following "Week against Child abuse."
That brought me back in touch with our old girl next door, and also with Cindy.
Her side of the story confirmed what I already knew, but because they often said that I lied and reality/fantasy couldn't separate from each other, I doubted myself

anyway. And that while I had felt the beating and had endured the pain.

However, at the end of her story, I was shocked:

While Nel told us that all children got away and the foster parents lost everything due to their crimes, none of this turned out to be true.

Cindy told me that they still lived there for at least 1.5 years. They said that I was crazy and therefore had to get hospitalized in a particular mental health clinic.

That made Cindy think twice because she knew I wasn't crazy; she knew what we were experiencing during living with these people.

She kept a diary with all the events,

She was now the oldest of the girls and got to take responsibility for my senior duties.

Eventually, all the children got away the moment Cindy opened her mouth. Our foster parents also did not lose everything, as had been told.

I held my first book presentation in the mall opposite the foster home. I told my father to take a walk upon the house where the tragedy happened, like a sort of moment of closure.

While I walked past the windows from our old bedrooms, I noticed the blinds were the same. I walked towards the entrance of the house and read the name on the nameplate.

I was shocked and my father too!

On the nameplate still showed their name.
Because of this, we suspect that Child Care has covered it up since it was their responsibility to check the foster home and guarantee the children's safety.

There are also many beautiful things happening afterward, like that I am gaining momentum from personal growth, and I have addressed my trauma through therapy and self-examination. I have grown enormously as a person.
I have learned to love, accept, and embrace myself.
My personal experiences and a considerable amount of theory to follow my passion in life grew.
I am proud to announce; I became a therapist, specialized in trauma processing, personal growth, and mindset.

I met the love of my life on Instagram, and I had to face my fear of flying in an airplane. I paid the first visit to him in India in 2016. After I learned to embrace myself, Lokesh came into my life, and we got married on 20 February 2018.
We work together in our practice, where he works as a personal trainer and supports body and mind programs for people who want to lose weight and a healthy lifestyle.
We also run a YouTube Channel called Singh In Holland, where we share our daily life with our viewers.

This way, our family and friends in India are always connected to us.

The fear of speaking in front of groups/cameras is also gone.

I provide lectures for large groups, and I plan to attend seminars for people who want to deal with their traumas and are ready to live their most beautiful life.

Everything goes well with my children. Everyone is happy and healthy, the boys are in their second year of high school, and the oldest is still doing great with his donor's lungs.

All my dreams came true.

Do you have the idea that you might need some help yourself? Have you experienced a lot, and do you want to find out how this influences your present and future? Do you find it hard to trust, or do you have low self-esteem?

Please contact me through
praktijkhappyenzen@gmail.com.

I provide online consultancy for international clients.

Love   Elisa   Singh-   Teulings

Printed in Great Britain
by Amazon